MW01295775

*"A Handbook for Healing and Restoring
after the Death of a Loved One"*

Presented To:

_____

From:

_____

Date:

_____

PRAISE FOR
HOPE: The other side of Grief…

As a pastor's wife and Director of Adult ministries, including Pastoral Care involvement at a large church for 15 years I have had first-hand experience in dealing with people that are grieving over the loss of a loved one. 2 Corinthians 1:3-4 says, "praise be to the God and Father of our Lord Jesus Christ, the Father of compassion and the God of all comfort, who comforts us in all our troubles, so that we may comfort those in trouble with the comfort we ourselves have received from God. "I heard this verse translated as saying, "Our troubles give us vocabulary to help others." Scott does an excellent job at addressing this very painful subject, with a "vocabulary" of gentleness, guidance and understanding of the Word of God and also the wide range of emotions people experience.

This is a must read for anyone going through a difficult time and also would be an excellent resource for church's and counselors.

Michelle Johns, Director of Assimilation Ministries
Victory Worship Center, Tucson, Arizona

Dedicated in loving memory of my son,

Robert Scott Bacon "Bobby"

(1989-1991)

This book is a tribute to
the wonderful,
unconditional love which
God created and
expressed through the
unrestrained love of a
little boy with a big heart!

Though his journey here
was short, he touched the
lives of many - forever.

HOPE

The other side of Grief

Scott A. Bacon

Hope: The other side of Grief…
"A Handbook for Healing and Restoring Faith after the Death of a Loved One"
© 2012 by Scott A. Bacon

Edited by Melinda K. Bacon

All Bible Scripture quotations noted NKJV are from the New King James Version Copyright 1954, 1958, 1962, 1964, 1965, 1967 by the Lockman Foundation

All Bible Scripture quotations noted NIV are from the New International Version Copyright 1954, 1958, 1962, 1964, 1965, 1967 by the Lockman Foundation

All Bible Scripture quotations noted AMP are from the Amplified Version Copyright 1954, 1958, 1962, 1964, 1965, 1967 by the Lockman Foundation

This publication is designed to provide information with regard to the subject matter covered. It is sold with the understanding that the publisher or author is not engaged in rendering any professional advice. If professional advice is required, the services of a competent professional should be sought.

Cover Graphic © bahrialtay-Fotolia.com
Second Printing

ISBN: 978-1493725410

Printed in the United States of America

CONTENTS

FORWARD

Life Happens! Indeed life happens to all of us and none of us are exempt. It crowds into the arena of our living unexpectedly and unannounced. It is especially the tough stuff, the hard stuff, those difficult circumstances and events that again come without any announcement and nothing is more difficult to handle than the loss of a child. The grief that it brings at times is overwhelming. The confusion that it can cause along with those feelings of despair can be so strong and at times so ruthless. The long and lonely nights, the difficult days that are so painful to navigate and indeed sometimes the pain seems to never go away. What is needed at times like that is not some quick fix or some superficial answer to the anguish and pain but rather someone who has been there and navigated such pain, someone who has real answers for the harsh reality of life and can provide insight and help to navigate those deep moments of grief.

Scott Bacon is one of those people; he has had his world turned upside down. Overwhelmed with the loss of that child he so deeply loved. Overwhelmed with the reality that he will never see that precious gift again in this life and yet by God's grace and help he was able to come out of the despair and now he writes with candid honesty and open vulnerability about his own journey through those dark painful moments. He has been through those long dark nights and he has journeyed through those hard days.

This book will encourage you and this book will give you the hope that you need that you can in fact get through what you are going through. Again his honesty and transparency will be both refreshing and in fact at times challenging. He will open his heart to you, you will hear his cry, you will feel his pain, you will understand that he does not speak from theory but from the painful experience of a loss none of us want to have to navigate. The experiences he has learned, the insights he gained and the truth of God's words that he has proved reliable and trustworthy will be a tremendous help and blessing to your life. He will be candid and comforting, honest and hope-filled. He won't gloss over his pain with some superficial answers or with some quick-fix formulas; he will tell you the truth. He will show you the eternal truth of God's word and how he worked it into the fabric of his own pain and his own journey.

When you have finished making your way through this incredible book you will be filled with a fresh new hope and hear the promises of God throughout its pages. You will discover that God himself understands your pain because He too lost a child. You will discover grace in this book, grace to persevere, grace to keep going, grace to keep on living and grace to allow the loved one you lost to still live in your heart eternally. It is not a book of theories or nice ideas, it is a book about reality and how God's grace and his eternal word will enable you to navigate the most difficult and painful of losses; the loss of a child. Let God use the words that Scott has written to heal your heart, to fill you with fresh joy and to give you a new beginning. I am grateful that Scott has allowed his heart to be open and to share his pain but also his victory and his triumph. I pray this book will be a blessing to you. I am thankful God has used him to heal even people within our congregation of their own deep, dark pain.

Pastor Zane Anderson, Senior Pastor
Victory Worship Center, Tucson, Arizona

ACKNOWLEDGEMENTS

Although it may sound a bit strange, I am very grateful for this experience even though, at the time, it seemed like my life was over. In an instant my life was changed and started down a horrific path I had never planned or imagined. Thankfully, God has always been there through this journey from hurting to healing and I cannot begin to thank Him enough for the valuable lessons I learned. All the way through, His loving and caring ways lifted me up and placed me on solid ground in Him when I was sinking fast.

My deepest gratitude and genuine appreciation goes to you my precious wife, Melinda who over the years has provided the emotional support for me to heal and develop the dream of a ministry that helps others when they are hurting the most. This book started as simple journal recordings while walking though parks and around lakes just to get the thoughts and emotions from my head onto paper. You then took on the challenging role of book editor and have been involved in every aspect of this handbook become reality. So many times you have comforted me through all of the tears and encouraged me to share these emotions no mater how difficult. I am so very grateful for you and your endless love and support through our fifteen years together; and we are only just beginning!

Finally, to you the reader who has either purchased or been given this handbook because your life has somehow been impacted by the death of a loved one. I hope and pray that it provides comfort and healing for your soul during this very difficult time in your life.

Please consider that my story of recovery can be your story too. Because God has restored my life and filled me with new-found hope, peace and even joy, I believe with all of my heart that He can do the same for you! I encourage you to take the first step of faith and begin your own recovery. Soon you will find a restored sense of hope that will extend into every area of you life!

INTRODUCTION

It's been said that your story of healing can be the inspiration for someone else's healing. Actually, that is one of the most significant reasons for writing this book. When someone listens to how another has worked through the devastating pain of losing their loved one, it can bring hope to those who desperately need it. You see, when I lost my son there was no support system in place. And after several years of healing I vowed to God that, with His help, I would help others who find themselves in that same situation. In short, my story of healing can become their inspiration for a hope-filled life with the help of God!

I can remember it like it was yesterday… It felt like someone reached into my chest and ripped out my heart! I couldn't even catch my breath. Did that really just happen? How can I go on?

Overwhelmed by so many serious questions and excruciatingly raw pain, I stumbled around for what seemed like forever, looking for the answers that eluded me as well as everyone else around me… Why my son? Who can help me? Where do I turn? What do I do next?
Everyday my emotions were all over the map ranging from numbness, depression and loneliness, to feelings of doubt and uncertainty. I had difficulty knowing how to feel at any given moment and the silent thoughts in my head only served to confuse me even more.

This book is designed to be a tool used in the healing process. By reading, mediating, and journaling on the subjects contained within it, you can move along the path to a new, healthy future of your own one day at a time.

The following material is what I have discovered on my journey, one that changed from confusion, grief and depression into a complete transformation, healing and a new beginning.

If you are exhausted and discouraged from trying to heal on your own, then this handbook is for you. I have found it is impossible to heal without the Healer – God.

I am not a psychologist or counselor. But while walking through my deepest pain, I ultimately discovered a renewed faith. During this healing process I have found some answers that you may be looking for too. I invite you now to open your mind to new possibilities, so please read on…

HOW TO BEST USE THIS HANDBOOK:

This writing is more than the recounting of a story, much more. This is written as a handbook intended to be valuable to each reader over and over again. It is laid out with certain elements designed to assist in personal recovery from one of the most difficult tragedies in life – the death of a loved one. We do not always know why life's storms come. But usually, after some time has passed, with personal reflection we can see some of the good that was accomplished. However, simply knowing this does not make it any easier to endure the grief and gripping feelings of loss.

Hopefully, some of the insights shared within these pages will benefit you in moving through the grieving process and into a place of peace. If you are close to a survivor of such a tragedy, they may help you to understand and support your friend or loved one as they progress through their own grief.

Inside this handbook you will notice several icons listed with the following headlines:

"Faith Tips" These are little notes in each chapter which are ideas, thoughts, or actions that can help ease the pain and shift your focus to something more positive.

"Encouraging News! Memory Verse" These scripture verses are included in each chapter and may help to pull you through tough times, assist you in letting go, or perhaps adjust your focus based on truths learned from the Bible.

"Simple Truth" These inserts offer a fresh perspective on the topic at hand, or something to be learned from it.

"My Journal" This page is left intentionally for you to write down any thoughts or feelings that come to mind when processing the information in the chapter or insights from the suggested scripture readings

Please take plenty of time while reading through this handbook and meditate on the scripture readings in an effort to allow God to speak to you in a way that only the two of you may understand.

Also, it may be valuable to re-read a chapter to try and pull more out of it, or learn something different because you are growing and healing in different ways each day.

It can also be very valuable to record your thoughts and feeling at the end of each chapter. This process can help you work through what is going on inside of you, even when it seems to make no sense at all. Later, when you re-read a chapter, you can then identify the point where you were, and compare to where you have come to. This will help you identify your progress, and give you important encouragement.

Lastly, whatever system works for you will be the best approach to take. Just remember to keep an open mind and know that ***you are not alone***!

Do not let a season of mourning turn into a life of mourning " *For I know the thoughts and plans that I have for you," declares the Lord, "plans to prosper you and not harm you, plans to give you hope and a future." Jeremiah 29:11*

* PART ONE *

Grieving and Hurting

Chapter 1

A Father's Story

It was Saint Patrick's Day, March 17th 1989 in an Army hospital located on Ft. Stewart, Georgia where **Robert Scott** "Bobby" was born. At birth he weighed 9 lbs. 4 oz., and was 22 ½" long. Everyone in the maternity ward remarked that he looked like big football player! All I knew was at that moment I was the happiest man on earth! Finally, he is here and he is healthy! Thank God!

His name was to be a surprise to my father-in-law, as he had been lead to believe that we were naming him Scott, Jr. I was standing beside the neo-natal nurses who permitted me to put on his first diaper in front of a huge window where my father-in-law was video recording every second. I grabbed a post-it note and stuck it on the scale in front of the window. He zoomed the camera in and started reading the note while taping, he read…9 lbs. 4 oz., 22 ½" long, and then in large letters "Robert Scott." At that very moment he realized his grandson was named after both of us and excitedly remarked "I _really_ like that name!" From that moment on, Bobby was showered with love like he was the only child in the universe.

All of the newborn natal tests indicated that he was a completely healthy bouncing baby boy and could go home from the hospital right away. Bobby was very healthy and active for the first 7 months, rating 95% on the pediatric development charts. He loved to play on the floor surrounded by toys, and would swing for hours if you let him! Bobby was a happy baby and was always smiling or giggling. Needless to say, he had lots of girlfriends!

Then when Bobby was 8 months old, he came down with an ear infection out of the blue. Mary (my first wife and Bobby's mother) and I immediately rushed him to the emergency room. The doctor put him on the routine regiment of antibiotics. But he had to keep changing the medications as the infection was not clearing up. Bobby was acting and playing normally other than some local pain in his ear which was to be expected. But the infection still remained.

Then about a month later we were terrified when overnight he became very jaundiced in his appearance (a yellow skin color), which was likely triggered by all the medications. They all contained sulfa based products which became increasingly difficult for his liver to process out of his body. Alarmingly, we discovered that he had been prescribed too much medicine for his body weight and for too long of a period!

Bobby was immediately admitted to the base hospital. After no improvement for the next few days, he was transported to the Medical College of Georgia (MCG) for extensive testing, including a (needle-type) liver biopsy. Seemingly the hardest part of the testing was waiting three weeks for the results! As a brand new Dad I was so nervous that it was hard to keep my mind off of it. During this time I was preparing for military deployment to Central America within days and had to try and stay focused on my job. I wanted to stay at the hospital with my family. But it was several hours away and duty called. So there was not a choice in the matter, and off I went to Honduras. It was comforting to me when my Superior (First Sergeant) told me that if we discovered that Bobby would need a liver transplant, he would insure that I was transported home immediately - even if he had to pay for it himself! I trusted him and took him at his word.

Then, to our worst fears the tests indicated massive liver scerosis <u>which was irreversible</u>! This diagnosis meant that there was a significant portion of Bobby's liver that was destroyed and could no longer function. Life for our family would never be the same again…

I was only gone a week when I received the news, Trembling and in shock I nearly dropped the phone and raced home from Honduras. My First Sergeant kept his word and with his help I was able to be home in only two days.

Our family immediately flew to Omaha, Nebraska where we met with a Liver Transplant Team at the University of Nebraska Medical Center (UNMC). Without delay, Bobby was placed on an organ donor recipient list and we were given a pager to notify us when a donated liver became available. Once the pager went off, we had to rush to the hospital within a matter of 20 minutes so Bobby could be prepped for surgery. The stress was unbelievable! I remember feeling very confused and nervous all at the same time. My mind whirled "what if _____ happened?", or something worse?! It was horrifying not knowing what to expect! I felt powerless and helpless to do anything but wait. Nothing like this had ever entered my mind and to say that I was terrified would be an understatement.

The transplant team was exceptionally helpful and tried to explain what was about to transpire. To an outsider the process would seem like any other surgery. But this was so very different. The liver team met with us several times over the next couple of days to walk us through every step of the transplant process. The team was comprised of numerous professionals including transplant doctors, gastro intestinal specialists, nutritionists, neurological specialists, specialized nurses and also a counselor to assist with the unbelievable stress on our family.

There were so many things to learn: surgery prep, breathing on the ventilator, intravenous lines, medications (for the rest of his life), re-introducing solid foods, extended hospital stays during recovery, and of course a hospital tour. All of this together was very overwhelming. Yet nothing could have prepared us for the next step.

They took us to see another child who had literally just rolled out of liver transplant surgery. He still had all the tubes and lines coming out of seemingly everywhere and was also on the ventilator. The image of this child was indescribable and so shocking that it frightened me to my core! My feelings overtook me and I started weeping uncontrollably even though I did not know this child! I was horror-struck while imagining that my son would also have to endure this procedure! I became lost in my own thoughts as they overtook me. His little body looked so frail and helpless. How could he ever survive after this? Why did he have to go through this? Snapping back to the present, it took

several minutes to finally compose myself and continue with the next part of the hospital tour. Fortunately, they took us to see some children who were already recovering from this surgery. I breathed a sigh of relief as I looked at them playing and spending time with their families.

Everything was now all set to go and we were just waiting for notification by pager that there was a liver available. That pager became most important; and was always with us everywhere we went! We felt ourselves checking it constantly to insure that it was on and working properly. Our car was back in Georgia. So in order to stay within a few minutes of the hospital everything we did was limited to locations we could walk to or take short taxi rides to and from.

It was an intense struggle everyday to keep our spirits up and not fall apart. Even though we felt prepared for the big event, the fear was ever-gripping and it was all I could do to keep my mind off of everything that was to come. I tried to convince myself that things would be normal again and then I would look at my son and sob when I imagined what awaited him. Bobby had no idea of the pain and fear that he was about to endure. As his father I felt like it was my responsibility to protect him and yet I felt completely helpless. The only thing that seemed to help my anxiety was getting alone and praying to God. I had not been paying much attention to God in the previous years. But boy, did I want Him to show up now!

In a matter of a few days, we received the notification and I almost dropped the pager. In merely minutes we arrived at the hospital just like we planned: and Bobby's liver transplant surgery began. The surgery lasted 14 never-ending hours and we were on edge the whole time. During the surgery the hospital suggested we go for a short walk to get some fresh air. I will never forget what happened next… While walking down the sidewalk, I was almost run over by a woman frantically driving this huge, old car and I noticed three children bouncing around inside without any seatbelts on. I remember thinking to myself that while we were trying everything we could to save our son's life, this woman did not care enough for her own children to even buckle them up! On the walk back to the surgery waiting room, I felt both infuriated and saddened by this event at the same time. I thought to myself how life can be so unfair sometimes and often not even make sense.

Finally, the Surgeon came to the waiting room and informed us that everything went well with the procedure and that we could see him in just a few minutes. Even though the liver transplant team had done their best to explain the whole process to us a few days earlier, nothing could prepare us for the shock of seeing our son engulfed in several intravenous lines, wires and tubes. Bobby would have to remain on the ventilator for several more hours while his body was recovering from the trauma of this most invasive surgery. As I gazed upon my baby through my tears of compassion and incomprehension, I felt indescribably relieved to still have my son to hold, and was hopeful that the worst was over.

We each took shifts holding him in a rocking chair. It took a nurse's help just to move in and out of the rocking chair because of all the lines and tubes. As each day passed Bobby appeared to improve and regain energy. We were on constant watch for each of the liver function numbers to reach certain levels. It may sound strange, but sometimes it was a victory for the day to have one blood test number either go up or down toward the normal range – baby steps! When his blood tests steadily improved we began to feel a sense of relief. It's hard to describe the strong emotions that are involved, and sometimes it felt like I was holding my breath and my tears for long periods of time: like suffocating in uncertainty. Many times while rocking my son in the ICU, I thanked God for saving Bobby and even pleaded to let me take his place. His life had only just begun! Somehow it seemed so unfair. As a parent I had dreamed up so many plans for his life and I wanted us to experience them together. Now I was wondering if they would ever come true and it wrenched my heart to the very core of my soul.

While in the hospital, the transplant team invited us to attend a support group meeting for recent transplanted patients and their parents. It was nice to meet others who understood our feelings.

We all discussed our stories, cried together and learned a lot from each other. It was very comforting to me, except for the surprise during the introductions where seemingly everyone was announcing that they had been transplanted more than once... some even three times! When I realized this, it terrified me! I kept it to myself, but little did I know how prophetic their stories would be.

Three days later, on Bobby's first birthday, we celebrated success of the liver transplant surgery. We had a party in the hospital's pediatric playroom, and several of the other transplanted children came to the party along with their parents, nurses, doctors, and surgical staff. For the first time since the surgery Bobby was permitted to eat solid food. So he chose the frosting on his chocolate Birthday cake! For a short moment life seemed to resume some sense of normalcy and then…

Just days later his little body rejected the new liver, and in a whirlwind he was rushed back to surgery for a second liver transplant operation. This surgery lasted 17 hours and felt even more tormenting for us to handle than the first one. For the first time we realized that there were no guarantees that his new liver, or any liver for that matter, would be accepted by his body. It was very discouraging to imagine and I quickly had to force myself to focus on positive thoughts. My emotions were like a yo-yo, sometimes even paralyzing me with fear.

This new liver, which was generously donated by parents of a 12 year old girl, was accepted much better by Bobby's body. Thank God for organ donors! They give the blessing of life to many people and deserve our deepest gratitude. As a matter of fact, Bobby was featured on a local news broadcast during the "National Transplant and Tissue Week" segment. They described how many children do not survive due to a shortage of available donated organs from other children, primarily because Doctors fail to ask families if they would consider donating during the trauma of losing a child. I am so very grateful to these giving parents who decided to donate. Another incredible detail I learned is that it is possible to transplant only half of the liver and it will grow along with the patient! God's masterful design of the human body is amazing!

Bobby's recovery in the hospital was an intensely stressful time and became a journey of healing that we took just one day at a time. There were good days and not-so-good days for Bobby and us. The hospital became our home for over seven months and there was never any guarantee that he would get go home. It is not common knowledge that this type of medical condition is so complicated. I assumed that surgery would be followed by a reasonable recovery, and then back to normal… But this was life-consuming! You can only imagine the stress on our whole family for such a long duration - emotional, physical and financial. Being military, we did not have much money and it took every penny to stay in hotels for a few weeks at a time. Thankfully, there was a Ronald McDonald House in Omaha and they permitted us to stay there every few weeks for three or four days before checking back into hotels again. Because the Ronald McDonald House operated on donations only, we could receive a financial break every few weeks. Thank God for the Ronald McDonald House!

By Divine appointment, I met a man named Larry in the adult liver transplant ward. He was a teacher from a small town in Iowa and was on his third liver transplant. We quickly became friends and adopted him as Bobby's "Grandpa Larry." We had countless long conversations and he had such a comforting way about him. It was a breath of fresh air to have someone to explain how it felt to go through these procedures. Bobby was not speaking yet so he could not tell me how he was feeling or when he was scared, and Larry's descriptions gave me some insight.

Larry explained that he was very frustrated because it seemed that whenever he was about to get released from the hospital, something would happen to prevent it. Meanwhile his wife back in Iowa was terminally ill with cancer and was told she only had a few months to live. The separation was almost more than they could bear and we prayed often for Larry to have a chance to be reunited with Barbara quickly. We also discussed how difficult it was for him to get his questions answered while the liver team made their rounds everyday. He said that it was a struggle to remember his questions while the team was there. So I agreed to help him by asking the team his questions while they were in his room. Then I quickly zipped upstairs to catch them with my own questions about Bobby's condition. Larry suggested that we use his truck during our stay if we would bring him the supplies that he needed (stamps, envelopes, etc.). This arrangement helped us both beautifully! As our relationship developed I also learned that Larry was growing frustrated with having to update his family on his condition everyday. So I started contacting his family with the daily updates on his behalf. It helped him not to have to re-live the anxiety while helping his family stay informed of his condition. The good news is that Larry did finally make it home in time to be with his wife for about a month before she died. Unfortunately, Larry died a few months later. I am honored to have known them both!

Finally, the day came when Bobby was released from the hospital to return home to Georgia! Everyone was thrilled to be home again after seven long months away! We were hopeful and happy to re-connect with friends and neighbors, return to work, and watch Bobby continue to improve. Even though we were home, it was not without challenges. Bobby was taking over ten medications that were given at several different times of the day and in specific order. Just to travel around town there were several syringes that had to be prepared ahead of time and kept cool until he was ready for them. Bobby's condition was so serious that if he went without one of them, or if it was given at the wrong time, it could kill him! The pressure to stick exactly to the plan was horrendous and seemed like a full-time nursing job just preparing and keeping track of all the medications. Bobby was usually a good sport and took his medicines without complaining. But there was one time when he was refusing to take the most important one. It was the only time I had ever become frustrated with Bobby and of course he did not understand why it was so important. Who could blame him for trying to say 'no' after all of the pain he had endured? I on the other hand, instantly became frightened that I would lose him or that he would again slip into seizures and my tears began to flow as I tried again and again. Then, finally, to my relief, he gave in and took the medicine. I think after a while of fighting me Bobby could sense my concern and realized that I was trying to help him and not hurt him. Sometimes a father must ask his child to endure some pain in order to help them…

In addition to preparing and administering his medications, we also had to keep an inventory on hand, as these types of products were not readily available. Many of them took awhile to get and were very expensive. One of the most critical medications was named "cyclosporine." Its job was to suppress his immune system so Bobby's body would not reject his newly transplanted liver. This product was produced in Switzerland; was light and temperature sensitive; and was over $500 a bottle! At that time Bobby was consuming almost 2 bottles a week! We were on constant alert to insure that this product was protected at all times until Bobby consumed it, or it would lose its effectiveness.

One of the conditions of Bobby's release from the hospital was that there were to be daily blood draws required in order for the doctors to monitor his liver and other functions. When I agreed to this in the hospital I had no idea of what they meant, and probably would have agreed to anything just to get Bobby home! The real story was that a catheter (broviac) was connected directly to one of the arteries in Bobby's heart and extended out of his chest with two rubber-capped ends allowing for needle draws. Everyday I would draw enough blood to fill up several smaller vials that were for different lab tests and then flush-out the caps. There were only a few minutes allowed to get to the lab at our local hospital. So I prepared all of the paperwork in advance. Many days it felt like I was defusing a bomb with only a few minutes to do it in! The pressure was overwhelming but I did what I had to and kept a brave face even when I was frightened on the inside.

There were so many life-and-death issues that became part of our "new normal" daily living. Probably one of the most difficult tasks that I had to perform for Bobby was his sterile dressing changes on the Broviac catheter. Every week I changed out the old dressing with a new one to prevent an infection, which had to be accomplished without any contamination. This meant wearing sterile masks and gloves while switching bandages, cleaning the area, and replacing the tape covering. My anxiety associated with infection from contamination was colossal! Because an infection growing directly into his heart meant certain death! Many times Bobby would ease my tension by grabbing my elastic mask, snapping it back into my face and laughing! There was no way that I could do anything about it at the time, as my hands were busy completing the sterile tasks required, and I think Bobby took advantage of that time for play. I was always comforted by seeing him goof around because he was surrounded by and subjected to so much pain on a regular basis. While I was freaking out because of the pain involved with peeling back the old bandage from his already-sore & traumatized skin! When he is finished crying, he would reach for my mask, snap it back in my face and then giggle! How funny was he?

Even with all of these new changes and adjustments we were relieved to be "home" again. It was fun for us to visit friends and catch up on things unrelated to the hospital which had become our world in recent months. I was happy to be back to work and resumed leading my team of Heavy Equipment Operators. In my heart I was hoping that we were through everything traumatic. But in the back of my mind I was uneasy and worried.

Then, surprisingly one morning just a few weeks later, Bobby had his first Grand Mall seizure. Instantaneously, Bobby's face turned blue and his mother started performing mouth-to-mouth resuscitation while on the phone with emergency workers. Again, Bobby was rushed to the local hospital. It was quickly determined that he needed to return to the liver team doctors in Omaha. The only way to get him there fast enough was to take an $18,000 life-flight from Georgia to Nebraska. In a matter of just hours Bobby was back in the same hospital that performed the previous transplants. In the blink of an eye it seemed that everything was reversed back to just before the surgeries. Except this time it seemed even more life-threatening because of the seizures. This particular trip was gut-wrenching as there was only room for one parent on the life-flight plane. So it was decided that Bobby's Mom would go with him and I would fly out the next day. Thankfully, ticket money was made available to us through our local bank who took donations to help with some of our family's medical needs. I was incredibly shaken emotionally with feelings of anxiety and panic – these were days before cell phones existed. I worried that Bobby might die before I even got to the hospital. It seemed like eternity before I finally arrived at the hospital the next day!

By that time everything had settled down some and the doctors had actually been able to record one of the seizures while in the hospital, which gave them valuable data to use.   However, it still took the team of doctors several days of testing to come up with a possible reason for the seizures and determine a course of action.

> *"All of this life-and-death turmoil had left us emotionally drained, worn out, and confused… Would life ever be normal again?"*

Now that we were checked back in to the hospital, it was as if we had never left. All of this life-and-death turmoil had left us emotionally drained, worn out, and confused. Would life ever be normal again? But the reality was that we were living a "new normal" and many of our questions could not be answered by anyone around us.

After a couple of weeks Bobby was finally permitted out of the hospital. But he had to remain in the local area just in case something came up again. So we stayed in town a few months longer which added extra financial strain; especially as our car was back in Georgia. It brought comfort to be close to the hospital. But there is no substitute for being "home." Finally, after Bobby's health stabilized, we were able to return home again. We never did find out what caused the seizures. But now we had medicine to hopefully prevent further re-occurrences.

Shortly after this last trip back home to Georgia, I was able to obtain a job transfer to Kansas in order to remain closer to the hospital, located in Omaha. The paperwork was an arduous process and we were elated when it was approved. It was an uphill battle to get acceptance from the base hospital as Bobby's medications cost over $5,000 a month (even in 1990). Actually, when the hospital commander initially refused to support the transfer request, my Father-in-law (an Army Command Sergeant Major) decided to meet with him personally to discuss why he was going to change his mind and accept this request! *You just can't mess with someone's grandson and get away with it!*

This transfer meant that we would finally live within a few hours of the hospital, which brought us much-needed peace of mind. The arrangement worked out very well for several future minor hospital visits and we were so thankful to not have to stay for long periods.

Now, Bobby was doing better than he had ever done and amazingly he was happily playing along side the other kids in the neighborhood! He even had a girlfriend across the street! We were relieved that he was doing so well and our hearts were thrilled that our son was able to have fun again! God provided a house with a full playground right in our own backyard! Bobby made up for lost time by spending every day there having fun until complete exhaustion: He also loved to ride behind me in his bike seat. I cherish the memories of the times when I would peek back and see him completely asleep with his head hanging down contently. After stopping he would wake up and excitedly plead for more riding just as if he had never drifted off! Those were such precious times to me and are still vivid in my mind to this very day.

There were additional factors complicating Bobby's condition, one of which is that he had to use sign language for communication, as his speech ceased to develop during the traumatic times. The other was that Bobby's immune system was suppressed by ant-rejection medicine. Because of this, he could catch a cold or virus from someone with a healthy immune system who was unaware that they were even sick. Bobby however, would show the signs of receiving that virus within a few hours. We had to be constantly alert to the danger this posed, which frightened us whenever Bobby was playing along-side other children. Kids are always carrying some kind of germs. Yet while this was potentially fatal to Bobby, how could we deny him the joy of playing with the other kids? It was a dilemma that we faced daily and which caused constant anxiety. After weighing all of the factors and risks involved, we decided to treat him as an ordinary little boy and not to keep him in some type of bubble, yet continue to do our best to protect him.

About a year later, a new liver transplant team was assembled in Richmond, Virginia at the University of Richmond Hospital. They soon became the number one team in the United States. Actually, the Doctor who taught the Doctor which performed Bobby's surgeries was in charge of this new team. It was a "no brainer" for us to relocate for Bobby's sake, given his delicate and complicated medical history. So we obtained a transfer to Richmond. During the transition, Bobby and his Mom stayed with her parents, while I relocated our household. It was difficult to say goodbye to the other house and neighbors, because we had some of our best times there and we were finally a "normal" family again. That year in Kansas was what I considered to be a recovery year for all of us. But now it was time for a new place and even better medical care. So off we went!

While visiting his grandparents Bobby did terrifically in his new environment! He became so spoiled that he got pretty much whatever he wanted: and nobody deserved it more than he after everything he had been through! I laughed when only a few weeks earlier Bobby's Grandparents stated that he would not be allowed to have his bottle while watching movies on their Italian leather couch. But when I showed up, there he was on the couch wearing his shoes, watching a movie and drinking his bottle of milk!

Sadly, after only a month there he was admitted to the hospital with some type of virus that was yet undefined. Once again, we were thrust back into a state of anxiety and fright. Many times, children with medically suppressed immune systems become exposed to viruses and the actual type can be hard to detect because the symptoms come on so suddenly. No, not this! Not Now! Life was just now improving and it was so painful to be thrust all of the way back to square one!

We were terrified when Bobby slipped into a coma as the virus proceeded to shut down his vital organs, one at a time. It was cruel to our precious baby and it taunted us threateningly. It began with the kidneys experiencing renal failure (which required constant dialysis): then a swollen heart. My own heart sank every time I looked at the thick, red tubes extending from my son into the kidney machine. I was gripped with fear that he may not recover this time. Tears filled my eyes and began to overflow as I silently asked God why? Why do these things keep happening to our son?

Finally Bobby was placed in a medically-induced coma; paralyzed and sedated so the doctors could keep him alive while trying to fight the virus that was killing him. When news got out that things had become this serious, several of our friends gathered with us in Bobby's room. We took turns reading to him or watching his favorite movies; Bambi and Jungle Book. He knew every word and every song in both movies. Holding on to hope, it felt to me like he was still listening during these moments. There were times when we would gather with friends at his bedside and hold hands while singing hymns or taking turns praying. I was so very grateful for our new friends and how supportive they were, especially since they barely knew us.

I tried to deny my fears which were telling me that this time he may not recover. It took every drop of energy in my soul to try and stay optimistic, when all around me my world was caving in. There were moments at Bobby's bedside, when I would wonder if he could really hear me and understand anything that was going on around him. Could he hear me? What was he feeling? What was he thinking? Did he know how deeply I loved and treasured him? Did he hear me plead with God when I offered to trade places, if only He would let Bobby live?

A few days later the horrific news came when the doctors told us that there was absolutely nothing more that they could do. They were out of options and had exhausted all of their resources. Now, we just had to wait and see if things improved, and try to keep Bobby comfortable with medicine.

Immediately after the doctor finished speaking, my heart dropped into the pit of my stomach… My worst fears had become reality! I thought to myself, how could this happen after things had finally started to get better? Simultaneously we all began to burst out in tears and sobbed together as a family for a long time. All of our lives revolved around this little boy! If he didn't make it how could we go on?

I wanted to be alone with God and get some answers so I went to the Chapel in the hospital. In a state of shock and disbelief, I felt numb and almost as if I was in another world. It didn't feel real. Alone in the chapel I pleaded with God one last time to either save my son or take him home. The pain of limbo was tormenting everyone, especially Bobby. After sobbing bitterly and pouring out my heart for what seemed like hours, I felt some relief that God heard my prayers and that He was answering them according to His plan. For the first time I was able to leave a Chapel without crying continuously. There was an unexpected, yet deep, peace in my spirit. And I just knew down deep inside that everything was going to be okay-even if we lost Bobby. God was <u>still</u> in control and I had to continue trusting Him even though things didn't make sense to me.

Our Last Day Together

When I think back to the very last day that I had with my son here on earth it seems like only yesterday. It was a Sunday morning and I was listening to Kenny G's "Breathless" during the 45 minute drive to the hospital. The morning time was set aside for Bobby and me alone; and we would be joined by other family and friend later in the day. Bobby was still being kept paralyzed and sedated by medicine and was on a blend of 14 meds in addition to kidney dialysis while breathing through the ventilator. In all the previous months of numerous surgeries and subsequent recovery periods; I cannot remember a time when there was this much effort being made to keep him alive. In the back of my mind, I was preparing for the worst. But on the outside I was trying to make the best of things. We spent the morning and afternoon watching his favorite movies, "Jungle Book" and "Bambi." Of course, we had already watched them enough to memorize every single line and every song. Even now, all these years later as I reminisce on my precious son, I still sing "Look for the Bear necessities", which I remember word for word☺. During the movies, I would talk to Bobby and reassure him that everything was okay, and that Daddy loved him very much. I told him how brave he was for enduring all the pain and needles. And I said that God was going to take better care of him than I could and told him that he would get to meet Jesus soon.

I was beginning to let go; to say 'goodbye.' I wanted to be sure to say everything he needed to hear before our time together here slipped away. Words cannot express how heart-breaking it was to be unable to look into his eyes or to feel him reach for me to be held. I wondered how difficult it was for Bobby to hear my voice and not be able to answer me or even look at me. It must have been so terrifying for him. My only hope is that the medicine which kept him sedated also kept him from understanding what was going on around him. As much as I wanted him to wake up and look at me, I also wanted to protect him from the pain and fear of slowly dying. I know it may sound strange, but I really felt like we were having the best quality time together, in spite of these complicated circumstances. During these times, Bobby and I were connected at the soul level and I was trying to savor every moment alone with him.

Later in the day we were joined by Bobby's Mom, Grandpa, and Grandma. We each took turns spending time by either reading to him, or listening to his favorite songs and singing along. We all tried to make things feel somewhat "normal" for the hospital experience while in this wait-and-see scenario.

By now, Bobby's heart had swollen to several times its normal size, and the doctors suspected that brain damage had already become evident. After an intense and painful family meeting together with the doctors, we asked some close friends to come up to visit with Bobby as we all knew he did not have much time left. We felt a deep gut-wrenching sorrow combined with a small sense of relief, knowing that Bobby was going home and he was not going to have to endure all this pain anymore. His suffering would soon end and he would be healthy at last in Jesus' arms.

Now that we knew the inevitable, we gathered around the bed, held hands, prayed for Bobby, and sang some of his favorite lullabies with the radio playing. He held on for several hours: and all the while we kept taking turns at his bedside individually saying our goodbyes.

Later in the day I was alone with Bobby when everything happened like a whirlwind! Suddenly, his heart rate dropped and his body temperature increased severely. He was dying right before my eyes! I hollered for the nurse to send someone to gather up the family, FAST! Unfortunately, the rest of the family did not return in time, as things progressed so rapidly. I remember leaning over my son and stroking his hair while holding his little hand. Then, I slid my arms around his body to hold him the best that I could and in an instant, he breathed his last breath and was gone...

Just then, the oxygen sensor alarm sounded a flat-line tone that to this day I will never forget. Unfortunately, the nurse had forgotten to shut off that last alarm as she had the others. Through my tears and sobbing, I looked at my son and I could tell by his blank stare that he was already gone. I didn't know what to do. What does a father do when his only son dies in his arms? So I reached over and closed his eyelids and said a prayer for him to go home to our Father in Heaven. Just then, his eyes opened again and I stood there shocked and amazed! He was paralyzed and sedated - this was impossible! Then, for the second and last time, I closed his eyes. I've come to believe that at that particular moment in time Bobby's spirit left his body to return home, to God. After months of courageously fighting to live, Bobby was freed from this life's sufferings at last. He moved home to be with Jesus on Sunday, September 25, 1991

While driving home alone that night, my grief gripped me so hard that I had to pull over several times, as rivers of tears filled my eyes and violent sobs consumed me. Bobby's struggle was over. He was finally free from pain – but I felt like my pain had just begun…

Bobby's funeral was by far the most devastating experience I have ever endured. From the viewing to the ceremony at the church and cemetery, every part of this was very intense. Yet it seemed so surreal almost like it was happening to someone else. When I looked at my little boy in his casket, it did not even seem real to me. It seemed as though he was still in a coma and at any moment could wake up and life could be normal again.

When I stepped out of the viewing for some fresh air, my eyes still pouring out tears, I looked up to Heaven and asked God for some kind of sign that my little boy was with Him and that he was okay. Just then, I noticed a bird's feather falling in front of me. I looked around and saw no bird, power lines, or even trees for that matter. I asked myself where this feather could have come from, and by this time the feather was right out in front of me. I didn't even have to reach for it. I simply held out my hand with my palm facing upwards and the feather landed gently in my palm! Perhaps some could explain this event away. But to me it was God's immediate answer to my desperate plea.

I took the feather home with me and placed it in a framed picture of my son. And whenever I pass by, it gives me some much needed comfort by reminding me that God answered my prayer. My son is home and God is always walking with me.

Later, during Bobby's funeral I realized about half way through the ceremony that I was holding back my tears and all of my emotions were being stifled. There were several fellow military attending, and we were programmed to be emotionless robots. At that moment, I said to myself "what are you doing… your son is in that casket! Cry if you feel like crying! Who cares if anyone sees you!" With that, all of my emotions burst forth like a dam giving way! I let the tears fall and did not pay attention to anyone else or their reaction. It felt healing for my soul to let go of the sadness and sorrow that had accumulated in my heart. It was a river cleansing away the grief. I am so grateful that I gave myself permission to be human!

As it turns out, I was not the only one holding back my tears. When I looked up all of the pallbearers and many of the guests were crying along with me. When a child dies I think it is especially unbearable because all of our plans and dreams for them just seem to vanish at once. Instantly they're gone and we are left feeling empty, confused and alone.

> *"There is something unnatural about parents outliving their children. When it happens, the balance and order of life is thrown into a tailspin."*

Fortunately for our whole family Bobby knew his destiny. He had even shown us where to lay his body to rest. Only a few weeks before he died, while visiting the historical cemetery and National Battlefield in Saint Petersburg Virginia, Bobby quieted everyone during the tour. Then in sign language, he motioned for everyone to stop talking and instead listen to the birds singing in a very tranquil part of this historic cemetery.

It wasn't until later, at the funeral home while trying to get past the pain of loss in order to make all of the arrangements, that we remembered this significant detail. This realization left no doubt in any of our minds that this was the place where he wanted to be buried. In fact, I believe that he had been preparing us for this event, by making this enormous and uncomfortable decision for the burial location easier for all of us. It was an absolute miracle when we discovered that there was a plot available with five graves in that exact area.

A few weeks after Bobby was laid to rest in this very tranquil place, I was there visiting as I did most days. For some reason I glanced at the ground and noticed that several deer and bunny rabbits had visited Bobby's grave. As I looked even closer I could see that their little footprints were everywhere! I couldn't believe my eyes! I instantly became overwhelmed and cried tears of joy. You see, Bobby's all time favorite movie was "Bambi." I remember spending hours watching that movie together! And we had memorized every single line and song in the movie. They were some of our most treasured moments together and

I will never forget them!

This is the love story of my son and me; and not a day goes by that I do not remember him and the joy that he brought to my life and to everyone who knew him. Bobby was pure, unconditional love – everyone who met him immediately knew this and loved him as a result. He loved us first, so we loved him… sound familiar?

I am reminded of a story about a man who was angry at God for not saving his son's life. He asked God "where were You when my son died?" and God responded by saying "The same place I was when my Son died!"

Fresh Perspective

As hard as this loss has been for me to work through in my life, it has also brought me much comfort to remember that God has already truly felt my pain and He understands me. Because He gave up His own Son so that you and I can live!

Now I am equipped with this specific experience which helps me to provide compassionate assistance to those who are struggling with the same issues that I once did. This instant credibility with grievers has opened the door to many peoples' hearts and taken down walls that once seemed impossibly tall.

Recently, I was listening to a morning radio show where the DJs had asked for people to call in with the answer to this question; "If you could go back to your teenage years and tell yourself something which could change your life, what would it be?" At first there were several callers who shared that they would tell themselves to work harder in school, treat others better, or enjoy childhood more, etc. But then I heard a caller say that even though she had a horrible life in her teens because she was a heroin addict and drove away all of her family and friends, she would not go back to warn herself about the outcome from this disastrous lifestyle. The reason she gave was that now she has the opportunity to work with heroin addicts in a rehabilitation project and she seems to be the only person they trust because of her experience.

Although it may seem strange to hear, I would not change anything that has happened to me either. Because these events have drawn me closer to God than ever before and also led to this ministry of helping others who have endured loss. I remember identifying with this caller and feeling that this was one more of many confirmations that I am doing the right thing by serving others in this way.

After reading this book and working through your grief, perhaps you too can envision something good that can come out of this tragic experience in your life.

Simple Truth:

We do not know how many days we have together. So we must treasure every memory that each day brings.

Faith Tip:

When times are seemingly at their worst and you are tempted to blame God, invite Him in and ask for comfort, strength and guidance for your heart, mind and spirit – He will surely provide.

Encouraging News!

Memory Verse: *Isaiah 55:9*

As the heavens are higher than the earth, so are my ways higher than your ways and my thoughts higher than your thoughts. NIV

My Journal:

What does this subject or scripture reading make you think or feel?

_____

_____

_____

_____

_____

_____

_____

_____

_____

_____

_____

_____

_____

_____

_____

_____

_____

_____

_____

_____

_____

Chapter 2

Fluctuating Faith

Faith is an interesting topic. When times are good it is so easy to say "yes, I have faith in God that everything will work out in my life." But, when we are thrust into challenging circumstances, it can be difficult to even recall the faith we once had… It is paramount to remember that God is ALWAYS with us, even through the tough times: and we can rely on Him even when things don't make sense in our lives.

You have probably heard it said the "You cannot have faith if you do not have hope." There is much truth in that statement, because faith builds on top of a foundation of hope. Hope is the bedrock upon which everything else rests. Faith is described in Hebrews 11:1 (NIV) as "Now faith is being sure of what we hope for and certain of what we do not see."

It is vital in your healing process to identify the hope in your life, and then build your faith upon that hope. There are numerous chapters in the Bible that speak about hope in times of adversity or desperation. The first one that comes to mind is the book of Job, which can be a difficult read at first until we understand just how strong Job's hope in God was. Even when those around Job were advising him to give up on God, he determinately stuck to his deep-rooted hope in God and was rewarded exponentially for it.

One of my favorite empowering verses of scripture and promises of God is found in Isaiah 40:31 (NIV) where it says "but those who hope in the Lord will renew their strength. They will soar on wings like eagles; they will run and not grow weary, they will walk and not be faint."

Leading up to my overwhelming experience of loss, I had always considered myself to be a good Christian, faithful husband, and loving father. What I discovered about myself is that while I knew who God and Jesus were, I was not engaging with the Lord in a personal, intimate way. It was head knowledge not heart knowledge for me all of those years.

Looking back I can see how much more comforting and healing it could have been for me if I had chosen to include God in all of the areas of my grief and unanswered questions by praying, reading scripture, and talking with other Christians. Instead, I kept things to myself and really struggled trying to understand why this happened to my son. The death of my son was incomprehensible. I mean, what parent imagines their child dying?

At the time we were just a normal young, 20 something(s) couple who were forced to deal with some of the most difficult and life altering decisions anyone could ever imagine. On one hand I was thinking that I was in-tune with God and He was watching out for us, and on the other I was questioning why we were going through this. I was so confused in my faith that every day was a completely different level of comfort or fear about what was happening. My faith at the time was not grounded enough to handle what my feelings and emotions were telling me. Often my emotions would become so overwhelming that I felt like hiding somewhere until everything got better. Sometimes the doctors would be talking to me and I would just sit there with a puzzled look on my face, trying to understand what they were explaining. It was as though they were speaking a foreign language that I had never heard and did not understand.

My faith was tested daily because it seemed like every time Bobby made some strides forward, it was followed by a setback of some sort. Then I would start wondering in the back of my mind, and even sometimes ask myself. "Did I cause this through something I did wrong?", or "Am I being punished for something?" My mind played tricks on me constantly. And because my faith was not developed and had not been tested until now, it was not strong enough to conquer questions like this or to provide much-needed strength, confidence and comfort.

During this whole lengthy and challenging ordeal, Bobby's mother and I prayed often; both individually and together. In all honesty neither one us was strong enough in our faith to pray with real confidence in God's goodness, and were not really sure what we believed. Most of the time we were simply afraid of what problem was next and how to deal with the seriousness of it all. The truth was that before this occurred neither of us had ever known a personal relationship with Jesus or were seriously practicing any level of faith. My thoughts now are that we were only praying out of a heightened sense of fear and pure selfishness, which is probably pretty common behavior for parents in this kind of situation.

We were seeking comfort and yearned for someone to tell us that everything was going to be okay. Let me tell you, simple words cannot explain how terrifying it is when a doctor tells you that your child may die… <u>TODAY</u>! It felt like I was fatally stabbed in the heart and the pain was unbearable. Nobody wishes to outlive their children, and it just doesn't make sense when it happens! I can recall many, many times that I prayed to take my son's place so he could live a healthy and fun life as any other boy. I think it's natural for any parent to feel this way, but at the same time I felt powerless. It was my job as his father to protect him, right? But I couldn't.

Fortunately, I can say that somehow I never blamed God for taking Bobby home. In fact, one of my last prayers while Bobby was still alive was that God would take him from this world of pain and comfort him. While it was one of the hardest prayers for me to let him go, it was also the only time I can remember leaving a hospital chapel without tears. This time I finally turned it all over to God for His decision and His will to be accomplished.

This prayer is still very vivid in my mind. I remember entering an empty, quiet chapel at the Medical College of Virginia Hospital and I knelt down with tears in my swollen eyes. The pain in my gut was intense from all of the stress. Then I sincerely and unselfishly asked God to either save Bobby by completely healing him, or to take my son home to Heaven. Again I must say, this was the only time that I left the chapel without any tears. I had a peace that I simply cannot explain. I gave it all completely to God and knew that His will would prevail, and that no matter how I felt, God was in control.

> *"This time I finally turned it all over to God for His decision and His will to be accomplished."*

It seems so easy now, several years later, to say this without question. But during the traumatic and tense moments surrounding this decision to let go, it took every bit of faith that I could muster to have enough trust that somehow God was going to take care of everything and He would make things okay for the rest of us as well.

Many times people fall into the trap of blaming God, when in reality He is the only true friend that we have: and we desperately need His help to guide us through the pain we are navigating. We have to remind ourselves that we cannot understand the bigger picture that is God's plan. While things may not make sense to us now, there may come a day when we can clearly see some of the reasons why this event happened when it did.
Usually, the root of the question "why" is really an expression of rage and protest, and is actually a way of blaming God. I went round and round in my head about this for months until I finally gave up on receiving an answer. Later in this book I explain more about a God box or brain file folder in which to place the questions we wrestling with. This was the one thing that seemed to work for me, and only by consciously handing the question off to God was I free from the agony of having to know "why."

Just to give an example of how confused everyone was about their own beliefs, Bobby's mother was raised in a traditional Catholic background and was trying desperately on her own to make sense of it all. She was concerned that Bobby would not go to heaven because he had not yet been baptized. I on the other hand, recognized that the Catholic baptism ceremony was really to secure a pledge by "God Parents" who promised to raise the child in the knowledge of Christ.
   My belief however, is that any child, especially because a child is not even conscious of sin, is blameless in God's sight and will be

immediately welcomed home to Heaven with open arms. That being said, in order to be supportive of my wife's views, I elected to go along with her desires for a baptism ceremony.

So, we assembled a complete and formal ceremony at the hospital. Our new friends from the hospital graciously served as proxies. They were "Grandpa Larry" (a fellow liver-transplantee), and "Grandma Elaine" (a hospital volunteer) who stepped up in a hurry! "Hurry" was the key word, as we only had a few short minutes while Bobby was taken off of the medical monitoring devices to complete the entire ceremony! I remember holding my son with a make-shift cap on his head that was covering dozens of electrodes which measured brain activity to monitor seizures. It was so painful to Bobby that he was crying helplessly during the entire ceremony regardless of my attempts to comfort him in my arms. It took everything I had in me to go along with this and not scream at my wife for putting him through this pain! Needless to say, we rushed through the formalities as his nurse kept motioning that we had to get him connected back on the monitoring equipment.

Earlier we had been given two religious medallions and holy water by Grandma Elaine. These items had come from Our Lady of Lourdes, France *(which tradition suggests have been blessed by the Virgin Mary).* At the time, and desperate for hope, I really believed that even this might make some kind of difference. One of the medallions was fashioned in the shape of Christ's head which I wore on a chain around my neck. We all were grasping at straws substituting religious rituals for a personal relationship with Christ. These were indeed confusing and uneasy times!

I now recognize that our son was already pre-destined to return to Heaven as a baby. His baptism, holy water, and blessed medallions were only a desperate attempt by two frantic parents who, confused about their own faith due to religious rituals, were trying to insure that their child would go to Heaven. Desperate people in desperate situations without a personal relationship with

Christ, simply do not possess the strength or wisdom to endure hardships by themselves. We need help from God to walk through the difficult times in our lives.

> *"Part of my journey is to learn how to use those tools more effectively and to share this truth with others."*

Fresh Perspective

Life can be painfully hard at times and not make any sense to us at all. During these times our faith is what carries us through. If it had not been for my faith, I could not have overcome the severity of losing my son. For me, taking alone-time with Christ, praying continually throughout my day, and casting all of my cares on Him are life-saving tools which still help me maintain peace and joy in my daily life.

For some people a leap of faith is required just to get out of bed in the morning; especially in the first days after a loss. Taking that first step can be the hardest but most rewarding part of moving beyond our pain and into healing. Please remind yourself regularly that God will meet you there at your first step and continue to sustain you throughout your journey in life. Just learn to trust in Him and cry out when the pain is more than you can bear. He promises that He will always be there for us in every circumstance.

A good visual exercise for faith-building is to picture something that you really want which is just out of reach; and in order to grab it you have to let go of what you are currently holding on to. It has been my experience that once you make the effort, you will receive the reward of your faith! The lesson here is to trust in God, let go of the pain, and grab onto the peace He has in store for you!

Simple Truth:

God is with you at every level of your faith, and what He wants for you is to move to higher levels.

Faith Tip:

When tragedy strikes, it is important to not blame God. These are times to lean on Him the most!

Encouraging News!

Memory Verse:

Lord You are good and Your mercies endureth forever! Psalm 100:5 NKJV

My Journal:

What does this subject or scripture reading make you think or feel?

_____

_____

_____

_____

_____

_____

_____

_____

_____

_____

_____

_____

_____

_____

_____

_____

_____

_____

_____

_____

_____

Chapter 3

Feeling Alone & Isolated

Probably one of the greatest stumbling blocks to healing is when a person feels that he or she is alone and has nobody to share their grief with. When we try and heal ourselves without the assistance of others, it is a daunting and even impossible task. No one is an island. There can be no healing without the Healer Himself (Jesus), being invited into the mist of your grief. Even counselors and therapists who have not experienced this kind of grief first-hand can only provide text-book answers which only scratch the surface.

So many people suffer silently because they feel like they have nobody to turn to. Even spouses can have difficulty relating to each other or truly connecting when they are grieving. They usually cannot comfort each other because they are both grieving in their own way, which leaves no energy or compassion left to give to the other. Sadly, others assume that couples can provide comfort to each other, when in fact they are worn out and have nothing left to give.

One way to protect yourself from falling into the trap of isolation and loneliness is to take advantage of offers by friends to meet with you in the weeks and months after the funeral. Most good friends will offer their availability to get together when you want to talk. The trouble is, many people who are grieving do not call their friends and honor those offers. In many situations families are surrounded early after the loss by others who bring comfort through listening, providing meals, having coffee together, etc. Then a few weeks after the funeral, everyone returns to their own lives and the phone stops ringing with offers to help. To complicate matters, it can be uncomfortable to call those same people and ask for help.

Please remember, there is no shame in asking for help throughout your grieving process! People really <u>want</u> to help; they just get busy with their own daily lives and they probably don't know how to support you. Be persistent and do not forget the ones who extended the offer to you. Call them and tell them how they can help you at that moment. Chances are there are plenty of people who would love to help, if you just ask them.

Another ingredient for healing is to get back out into life and find something to get involved in. You may try volunteering somewhere, joining a group of some sort, or perhaps even just enjoying the outdoors. You will be surprised at how your spirit can be lifted! Believe me this is good advice and only after hitting emotional rock-bottom did I learn how to do things differently.

Even a little over a year after Bobby vanished from my life I thought I was strong enough to handle most things again. I quickly learned that many tender areas remained in my heart and I was going to have to find a way to deal with them. I thought back to an earlier time shortly after Bobby died. I was attending a grief group meeting, and when parents were taking turns introducing themselves, they were also stating how long it had been since their child died. Surprisingly, most had died 3-10 years earlier. In my mind I was rationalizing that I would be strong enough to move on in a year or so…. fat chance!

Then, against the Doctor's recommendations, the U.S. Army decided to send me on a one year hardship tour of duty to Seoul Korea. They call it a hardship tour because you are deployed without your family, or even a vehicle for that matter. All I was permitted to take along was 500 pounds of personal belongings. It had only been about 18 months since Bobby died and I was still raw emotionally. Many days it was all I could do to get out of bed and report for work. It seemed too early in my grieving process for a change of this magnitude; but orders were orders.

It did not take long for me to feel desperately alone and fighting depression became a daily ritual. Many days were complicated by the lack of spending money, as I was a soldier and most of my pay was used to provide for my family back home. There were very few things I could do or places to visit at little or no cost to help keep my mind occupied with thoughts other than my deep loneliness. I desperately wanted to be around other people, and even strangers were better than isolation.

Returning to live in the barracks environment wounded me deeply as I was accustomed to living with my family in a home. Finally, I found an opportunity to move off the military base and live among the local Korean people. It was a difficult process which required several forms and approvals. But I stuck with it and made it happen. It was great refreshment for my soul to have a new place to live, and there was a lot to see while walking around the city. The only down-side was that after the dust settled, I was alone again. It was extremely hard to make friends because most people were either coming or going as this was a place of transition for every soldier. What made it even more difficult was trying to relate with the people around me because they were either married with children - in which case the death of a child was the very last thing they wanted to discuss - or they were single and hanging out at the bars. Either way, I felt like an outcast.

For some comfort I started to read a variety of books to keep my mind off my loneliness. I began reading portions of the Bible and other inspirational books like one of my favorites "The Power of Positive Thinking," by Norman Vincent Peale. What I discovered is that while reading helped me to escape temporarily, I preferred to walk around and find something interesting to see or do in lieu of just sitting still.

Another trick of mine was to catch the bases' free shuttle bus to the golf course up in the mountains and spend some time in meditation. I could walk along the meticulously groomed fairways and spend hours appreciating nature. Occasionally, I would bring my golf clubs along when I could afford to play a round, or maybe just visit the driving range and putting green.

In the days before email, it was telephone calls that helped tremendously. But I had to use my calling card sparingly as air time was over a $1.50 per minute. Many times it was difficult to just walk by the telephone booths while fighting the urge to call home for a friendly voice. I finally saved up the money to purchase a fax machine which was faster than mail, but cheaper than calling. The mail took over a week in each direction, so the fax machine was a valuable asset to my staying connected to everyone "back home." It's funny how fast a call back home can pick up your spirit! I'm not sure what I would have done without it.

These were indeed strenuous times in my life. Mornings were the hardest time of the day for me. I can still recall that on many days as I was walking to work, for comfort I would hum the song "this little light of mine" just to make it through the day. Sometimes the pain became so hard to bear that it would just sink into the pit of my stomach and I didn't even want to live anymore. There were many days when I would sit in a swing on the playground at one of the base schools and start to ponder troubling questions like why I was even alive? What was my purpose here? What do I have to live for? Does anyone even care about me?

> *"Sometimes humming a favorite hymn or song can keep fear at bay and remind you that God is close by."*

It was such a shock to my system to feel this alone and isolated. I was accustomed to having people around me and plenty of things to be doing to distract me from my pain and all of the questions that plagued my mind. Now there was nobody around me that I knew and seemingly nothing to do to take my mind off everything and everyone that I was missing. Inside my thoughts were screaming "help me," or "please talk to me!" But without the ability to verbalize these thoughts, nobody around me had a clue how I was feeling.

One cool and sunny afternoon while sitting in a schoolyard playground I remember asking God "What do You want me to do?" I was so depressed I didn't really even care if I lived or died anymore. In all honesty, the only thought that prevented me from considering suicide was that I did not want to risk losing the opportunity to reunite with my son in Heaven. I was concerned that if I interrupted God's plans for my life, that I risked eternity without my son.

This period of time in my life was probably the most pivotal and confusing. In the blink of an eye, everything had changed and now I was a dad without a son – I kept asking myself what purpose I even had anymore! There was this persistent and massive knot in the pit of my stomach that wouldn't go away. Every time I walked by the picture of my son I would get an overwhelming feeling of sadness that made me want to curl up in a ball and just disappear. All I wanted was to feel my son in my arms again! In my minds eye I could see him running towards me when I returned from work, or playing peek-a-boo, which was his favorite game. My mind had so much trouble grasping the brutal, instant life change from being part of a loving family to being isolated and alone. To make matters worse, there wasn't even anyone around me that I could talk about how hopeless I had become. The psychologist assigned to me had nothing to offer as he had no experience with grief like this.

Then, while sitting in that playground I heard a voice inside tell me to get up and walk across the street. I cannot explain what kind of voice it was, only that I heard it unmistakably. When I summoned up the courage to get up and actually walk across the street I discovered a facility which I had not noticed before that was named "Child Services!" I had not recognized the name of this military facility and had no idea even what it was. When I entered the building I noticed a large reception desk and behind it were several children of different ages who were playing video games, ping pong, and reading. Just then a manager stepped up to greet me and asked if I had any questions. The first thing I inquired about was what they did there, and he explained that they took care of children after school until their parents could pick them up after work. As military and civilians working for the military, many parents had unique schedules and this was a terrific way to insure that their kids were safe and kept occupied until they could return. It went beyond what you would expect of a normal daycare facility because there was much more interaction between the volunteers and children.

To my surprise, he also mentioned that they were very short-handed at the moment and could really use another volunteer. I stood there dumbfounded and pretty confused about what to do or how to answer him. Before I could even think it through, I opened my mouth and said "yes, I'll be glad to help!" In an instant something told me that I had made the right decision. In fact, I believe this was the healthiest decision I made while stationed in Korea!

Before long I was reading or playing games with the kids several days a week. Occasionally a few other adults and I would take the kids roller skating, which was so much FUN! The next thing I knew, I was recruited to be a soccer coach! I coached a team of fifteen 8 and 9 year old children. What a blast! It was a challenge at first: but after I laced up my own cleats and really started teaching them it became much easier and a lot more enjoyable. With practices two nights per week and games on Saturday, I really began looking forward to these times so I could keep my mind in a happier place.

What made it so enjoyable for me was that I was around kids being kids again. I will never forget during one of our games, I turned around to look at our Goalie; and there he was with his arms entangled in the goal net after goofing around when he was bored. It was hilarious! Some Coaches would have lost their minds, but I just started laughing hysterically!

> *"These kids had no idea how much they helped me through some very tough times in my own life!"*

By far the most memorable time was our final pizza party at the end of the season. The parents secretly passed a "Thank You" card around for all of the kids to sign along with a gift certificate which they presented to me. I still have that card with all of their signatures in a picture frame. When I look at each name I can still picture their faces even all of these years later. It gave me such great joy to make a difference in their lives and these kids had no idea how much they helped me through the most painful time of my life! God is great! And He works through some of the most unsuspecting people. Thanks to these experiences and relationships, I was able to deal with the pain and feel less isolated. Before long, it was time to return to the US and begin a new chapter of my journey.

Fresh Perspective

You may want to consider setting aside a specific amount of time to mourn; to permit yourself to truly feel, grieve , and process your loss. Don't force yourself to be super-human. Be gentle with yourself and let your tears and thoughts flow. But be sure to promise yourself a deadline for <u>when you will embark on the journey of recovery</u>.

Ancient laws prescribe <u>40</u> days for mourning according to Genesis 50:3 and the Egyptians extended it to <u>70</u>. This can be a guideline for you; as it has been a proven approach throughout the ages. But remember to do whatever feels right to you with the ultimate goal of moving from mourning to healing.

In my loneliness I was clueless that God was with me every step of the way... Looking back now I can see that He was carrying me through those times, much like the Footprints poem you may have seen. The poem talks about a troubled man who is walking along the shoreline and looks down to see that two sets of footprints have now turned into only one set. This bothered the man. So he asked the Lord, "Did you not promise that if I gave my heart to you that you'd be with me all the way? Then why is there but one set of footprints during my most troublesome times?"
The Lord replied, "My precious child, I love you and I would never abandon you. During those times of trial and suffering, when you see only one set of footsteps, it was then that I carried you."
Author unknown

I have learned over the years that God is indeed with me and when I get alone with Him for prayer each morning, I can feel His presence: and on the occasions that I can't, experience has proven to me that He is still there. These times are so precious to me that I can count on one hand the number of times that I have left the house without taking time with Him. I imagine Jesus holding my hand while I pray and His presence provides the strength and confidence I need to get motivated as He reminds me that He has something for me to accomplish each day. He gives me purpose!

I double-dare you to try it for yourself! I know you will find your own peace, comfort and strength in the arms of our Savior…

Simple Truth:

We may _feel_ all alone, but the truth is that we are never really alone at all.

Faith Tip:

Surrounding yourself with others frequently can ease your pain and give you something to look forward to– there is no room for sadness, when others are lifting you up!

Encouraging News!

Memory Verse:

For I am the Lord your God who takes hold of your right hand and says to you, do not fear, I will help you. Isaiah 41:13 NIV

My Journal:

What does this subject or scripture reading make you think or feel?

Chapter 4

Longing For Belonging

It is simply part of our human nature to want to be connected with others and to be part of something. Often we will go out of our way to spend time with friends or family and even travel great distances to be with them. One significant change that happens when our children die is that we experience something many others cannot relate to. This can make it a challenge when communicating with others, both individually and in groups.

It is perfectly normal to want to express our feelings to others. But the difficulty becomes how others will react to this kind of information. There can be a shift in the relationship, as others do not know how to react or what to say. Consequently, they can become uncomfortable and can even shy away from us once they hear our story. When and if this happens, it is vitally important to remember that even though the situation is different, it does not mean that anyone is bad or wrong. In general, people have a tough time adjusting to dynamics that they do not understand. It can take extra time for people to process the seriousness of the information that you are sharing with them. You may even feel that there are only certain people you can trust with this information; and that is perfectly normal.

Something to consider when seeking a new friend or a group is to insure that they accept you for who you are, and have compassion for what you have gone through. If they cannot accept that, then it may not be the right relationship or group for you.

Thinking back, one of the most difficult road blocks to my healing process was that I did not really feel grounded anywhere. Everything was in a constant state of flux and I was void of someone close enough to trust with my feelings. It seemed that no one around could possibly understand my loss or confusion about not having a family anymore. During my deployment to Korea, I became legally separated from my first wife, due in part to our grief and strained emotions. Now, I had lost <u>all</u> of the family that I had been close to; my mother-in-law and father-in-law, spouse and son... talk about an excruciatingly painful and confusing time! Some days I felt like my life was okay and everything would work out. Then other times I didn't feel like living another day.

Toward the end of my one year tour in Korea, the time seemed to drag on endlessly. Being a soldier in a foreign country is a lonely assignment. I felt like I had no one that I could really talk to about my feelings. Every time I reached out to someone who seemed like they might become a good friend, I was afraid to really be myself.

So much of my life seemed to be about these intense and severe subjects that nobody else could relate. How is it possible to get involved with others and not share who you are with them? It was really a difficult state from which to build relationships.

In an attempt to reach out and find comfort, I began to attend a local church. There I met many terrific, well-intended people. But again, I was the odd-one-out. It was always the "elephant-in-the-room" kind of issue. Who could I possibly share my thoughts and feelings with that could understand or at the very least, be sympathetic? Another hurdle was connecting with someone who had a similar experience. It was difficult to find others who could empathize, as this was not exactly a light topic for dinner conversation. It seems to me that there are many more suffering people in our midst than any of us realize. To that point, now that I am strong enough to share this part of my life with strangers, I am constantly discovering more people in both my personal and professional life that have experienced the same kind of loss. As a matter of fact, I believe that God has placed these other parents in my life to help me heal by my providing comfort to them and to motivate me on the completion of this book.

> *"I am constantly discovering more people in both my personal and professional life that have experienced the same kind of loss."*

After leaving Korea and before arriving at my next duty station in Fort Leonard Wood Missouri, I took a few weeks to visit my Mom and Dad. They of course we're very glad to see me back in the United States and if felt good to be around family again. Even though they could not completely understand how I felt, it was good to be able to share my feelings in a safe environment. The real irony is that now (years later) they can understand all too well, as my youngest brother died at the age of 33 and my sister died a few years later at 50. Of course, after that event they were full of questions of there own. Even with adult-children the pain of losing them early is traumatic. As I mentioned earlier, it is not normal for us to outlive our children and it is very challenging to wrap our minds around.

After a short visit with family, I reported for duty in Missouri. Again I found myself in an empty home, new job, and absolutely no friends. Boy was this routine getting old! My only moral support came from an Army Psychologist, who after hearing all that I had been through could only say how surprised he was that I was holding together so well! While this was encouraging, it wasn't very helpful in getting me through these very painful, lonely. and tumultuous times. I was shocked that this was the only comment that he could make! Obviously he couldn't provide anything useful for me, which only made me feel like I was on my own again. To be fair, I am sure he thought he was cheering me up. But he wasn't. For me, medication was completely out of the question. Medication only dulled all of the senses, made me feel lethargic, and definitely did not permit me to process the deep grief I felt inside.

During these times I started to read the Bible and pray. Unfortunately, I was in a very remote area and there really were no churches to choose from. Occasionally I would visit one near my home on post, but never felt welcomed or comfortable. Even though I tried to reach out it seemed everyone was quite into their own lives. Once again it was difficult to get connected, as most of the members were in the military. Often, people in the military are constantly on-the-move and may not want to connect with others because they expect to move again soon.

It's the same old story again. The real quandary was that when I was among families I had to share at least part of my story, which they definitely were not ready to hear. And the singles groups were too young to understand. Either way I was lonely and alone.

When trying to relate to others, probably the most significant factor is that a paradigm shift is inevitable whenever they learn you've lost a child. The interesting part of that statement is that I was the only one who knew the story ahead of time. The result was that I remained silent much of the time to avoid this whole disruption in everyone's lives and so I could never really develop true friendships. This problem really only magnified my pain and later became a big part of why I wrote this book.

Fresh Perspective

 Continually remind yourself that you are not alone! Feeling like you are alone or that your loss is unique is probably the most damaging thought a grieving person can have, and many times drives people into isolation which is *not* the answer. In fact, it makes the grief worse!

Once we really start to look around we quickly discover that there are *many* people we come in contact with in our daily lives who have experienced losses and are silently wondering if they, too, are alone. While it is true that in our lives we will all experience losses at some point in time, we do NOT have to go through it alone!

Keep reaching out until you find someone who accepts you for who you are and what you have gone through. God can make a way to connect you with others who share this experience and provide the safe, open opportunity for the sharing of your story. In fact, my wife and I have started a healthy grief recovery group in our area and soon will be expanding into other cities and states. We are honored to be able to offer a link to several recovery resources through our website. Please visit www.hopetheothersideofgrief.com for more details.

Simple Truth:

It is important to remember that we are never truly alone, even though it feels like it at the time!

Faith Tip:

Sometimes when I was feeling very alone, I would quietly sing "This little light of mine."

Encouraging News!

Memory Verse:

God is our refuge and strength, and ever-present help in trouble. Psalm 46:1 NIV

My Journal:

What does this subject or scripture reading make you think or feel?

_____

_____

_____

_____

_____

_____

_____

_____

_____

_____

_____

_____

_____

_____

_____

_____

_____

_____

_____

_____

Chapter 5

Slipping Backwards

Sometimes life can feel like a gigantic roller coaster with many twists and turns we can't see coming! On several occasions, I have experienced the sense of slipping away from God's hold on me during the craziness of life. Every now and then it is far too easy to be drawn towards the everyday things of this world, some of which are not very healthy at all.

Temptation can be very powerful and luring. But in the long run always proves to be detrimental to our relationship with God. He wants us to be obedient and remain true to Him; which is for our good as well. I find it helpful to think of God as the "Perfect Parent." So many scriptures make even more sense in light of this perspective. God gives us free will to make our own choices - good (helpful) or bad (unhelpful). He is always there to guide us without forcing us in one direction or the other. It must feel wonderful to God when we choose to be obedient and follow His leading. In that very moment we can feel so much closer and totally connected to Him! I can imagine Him shouting "YES!" from Heaven's throne as we make the right choice! If I only had realized this revelation sooner in my life I could have known much more comfort, joy and peace without struggling so much.

When I returned from over-seas, I found myself again living alone in a new city with absolutely no close friends; and it was a daily struggle for me just to stay optimistic. Friends can be so important to us by providing that "constant" when everything else is fluctuating. Now I can look back and see that God Himself has always been my constant companion, even though I was pretty much unaware of His presence at the time. Scripture reminds us that He will never leave us or abandon us and that He longs to be involved in every aspect of our daily lives.

In my new environment I was presented with numerous temptations, both good and bad. Several times I made poor choices and experienced some very challenging relationships which proved to be unhelpful to my recovery. During those times I could feel myself slipping away from my faith, mostly because I was embarrassed by my wrong choices and was feeling convicted on the inside. It was a subtle kind of feeling where you know something is not quite right, but you keep doing it anyway until it becomes very obvious that it was truly the wrong decision and the wrong person.

> *"That the feeling in my gut was really God telling me to trust Him and hang in there… there were much better days ahead…just trust and believe."*

Being newly divorced and feeling very alone seemed to make a way for an even more promiscuous attitude. I lowered my standards in order to have relationships, whether just friends or more intimate.

The truth in these situations was that the feeling in my gut was really God telling me to trust Him and hang in there… make better choices… there were much better days ahead…just trust and believe.

Life for me was off to a new start, but what did that mean? How does anyone start over after something like this? For that matter, how do you even go on living? I've never known anyone who lost their child and their marriage. Where could I turn for answers?

> *"It was not so much the attention that I was after, but more a feeling of wholeness when you are really close to someone."*

After a while I began feeling desperate for an intimate relationship because at times the loneliness was almost unbearable. Of course, everyone knows that we don't always make the best relationship choices when we feel desperate. It was not so much the attention that I was after, but more that feeling of wholeness when you are really close to someone. The trouble was that I could never find someone who could understand the *new me* and accept me - "baggage" and all.

Many times I have heard it said that we have a "God-shaped" hole in our heart and we try and fill it with anything we can think of instead of God. But until we seek Him for who He is, and allow Him to come into our heart we will never be truly satisfied. I am so grateful that He is patient and forgiving!

It can take much time and patience to get back to doing the right things. Even though I was giving up on myself and my future, God was not! What I needed to discover was a renewed purpose in my life, a reason to get out of bed every morning. My plans had been shattered and I desperately needed some direction on establishing new plans and goals for the rest of my life. Without a strong sense of purpose it is almost impossible to set goals in order to accomplish anything. The next two sections of this book will assist you in discovering and releasing new-found potential for your own future, through life-transformation.

Fresh Perspective

A very wise and dear friend of mine who is also a Pastor, Counselor, and noted Author described it best when he said "In any relationship, we are either growing together or apart at any given time. It is ALWAYS one or the other." It is also true that if we desire to turn in the direction of the other person we can catch up rapidly. This means that with a change of heart, we can work together and therefore grow closer very quickly. I believe this philosophy to be very accurate and true in my own life. Even in recent days, when I feel that my relationship with my wife or with God has become more distant, all I have to do is focus my thoughts and actions toward that relationship and the closeness resumes. It's really just that simple.

The key is to recognize *early* on that we are starting to drift in our relationships and make a strategic effort to focus freshly on that relationship and very quickly things will improve.

I urge you to try this approach on your own relationships and see how wonderful the results can be! Godspeed

Simple Truth:

God meets us where we are. He never Judges us and He does not hold our past mistakes against us.

Faith Tip:

Try a change of scenery. Changing your inner circle of friends can bring you to a higher standard.

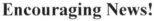

Encouraging News!

Memory Verse:

Set you minds on things above, not on earthly things. Colossians 3:2 NIV

My Journal:

What does this subject or scripture reading make you think or feel?

_____

_____

_____

_____

_____

_____

_____

_____

_____

_____

_____

_____

_____

_____

_____

_____

_____

*PART TWO *

Transformation

Chapter 6

Coming Back to God – My Personal Testimony

What a beautiful and enlightening moment when I came back to God!

A personal testimony does not need to be complicated, it's really just "your story" told in your own words about how you connected or re-connected with God our Father. One reason testimonies tend to have such an impact is because of all the passion that is tied up in the story. Nobody knows your story better than you and when you share it with someone it is impossible to hold back the emotions invoked by the experience.

It's been said that your story of healing can be someone else's prophesy. Actually, that is one of the most significant reasons for my writing this very book. I believe that when someone listens to how I overcame the devastating experience of losing my only child, it can bring hope to others who desperately need it. You see, there was no support system in-place for me when this happened and after several years of healing, I vowed to God that with His help I would like to help others who find themselves in the place where I once was. In short, my story can become their prophesy for a hope-filled life through Jesus Christ!

For the two years after Bobby died, my relationship with God was not at all close; mostly because I was not thinking or acting like the man I could have, and really should have, been. Then an incredible thing happened! One of my clients had just become an ordained Pastor at a local church. A co-worker who was a member of that same church asked me to lend some moral support by attending the Pastor's first "official" service. It just so happened that, unbeknownst to me, this particular service included baptisms of several newborn children. Suddenly, a procession of families filed out onto stage for their turn at the baptismal. One at a time they would give a short speech about how the Lord came into their hearts and had changed their lives forever. I was keeping my composure perfectly well for a while until the Pastor approached a family with a young baby. I tried my best to hold the emotions inside, but couldn't any longer. Soon I began to cry to myself and was trying desperately not to embarrass the co-worker's teenager sitting beside me. Finally, I could not hold back the strong emotions inside and I just broke down and let it all out! What liberty to let it all flow at last. I began to thank God for getting my attention, started praying, and gave my life to Christ right then and there! I accepted Jesus into my heart and made Him my Lord and Savior!

> *"If God is your co-pilot, you better change seats!"*

I realized shortly afterwards that only God in His infinite wisdom knew how to get my undivided attention. He lined everything up that evening to finally break through my armor and remind me that I need Him for everything in my life. He is the One who must be in control of my life, not me. My life is His alone and He has a plan for me. In Jeremiah 29:11 God says "For I know the plans I have for you, declares the Lord, plans to prosper you and not to harm you, plans to give you hope and a future." I cling to this scripture and it fills me with hope to keep going even through the valleys in my life. Just remember that God is ALWAYS in control – He is never surprised by how you feel or what you are going through. He is truly the only constant in all of our lives. We just have to recognize that fact. I once read a bumper sticker that summed it up very well. It read "If God is your co-pilot, you better change seats!"

God has a pre-planned purpose for each of our lives and He wants to share that with us. The Bible reminds us that when life's difficulties and tragedies happen, they can bring us closer to God by forcing us to constantly lean on Him to make it through our daily challenges, large and small.

The back side of a tapestry is a great reminder of how God works and all of the connections that He makes. When you look closely at the back side you will find threads stretching seemingly haphazardly all over the place. While this may look like complete chaos, flip it over and you see a perfect picture woven on the other side.

> *"God has a purpose for each of our lives and He wants to share that with us."*

Ever since that day I accepted Christ, my faith has grown exponentially! It hasn't always been easy. Because in order to start fresh I had to end a few relationships with some friends that were bringing and keeping me down. Remember to take an inventory of the people around you and ask the question, "are they lifting me up, or bringing me down?"

One significant point which I have learned in life is that when catastrophic events transpire, it forces us to make some pivotal decisions about how we will choose to live our lives going forward. I call them "life-defining" moments. We all have them; but unfortunately they are not always dinner conversation. So they tend to go unspoken or unnoticed.

Fresh Perspective

A while ago, I was reading some scripture in Mathew and I realized that the <u>loss</u> of Bobby (my son) is "my cross." The scripture read *"Then Jesus said to His disciples, "If anyone would come after me, he must deny himself and take up his cross (burden) and follow me. For whoever wants to save his life will lose it, but whoever loses his life for me will find it" (Mathew 16:24 NIV).* Even though this loss has been my personal burden, it has also defined who I am choosing to become. This experience is both the worst and best thing that has ever happened to me. As difficult as this journey has been, I would not change anything. Because now I have the tools to help others! That is why I delight in sharing this book with you! I have chosen to help others regain hope and to begin healing through fuelling their faith. Yet, through giving to others I receive much more in return than I can possibly convey. Not only does it aid in my own healing; but it brings me closer to God, our Supreme Healer. And, closeness to Him is the *ultimate* reward!

Simple Truth:

My life has not ended, my life with You (God)
it's just beginning.

Faith Tip:

Developing a humble heart and accepting the help
that only God can give you will bring us back to
Him and can provide a renewed sense of peace in
our lives.

Encouraging News!

Memory Verse:

Blessed is the man whose sin the Lord will
never count against him. Romans 4:8 NIV

My Journal:

What does this subject or scripture reading make you think or feel?

_____

_____

_____

_____

_____

_____

_____

_____

_____

_____

_____

_____

_____

_____

_____

_____

_____

_____

_____

_____

Chapter 7

A New Beginning

My hope is that you are able to experience a new start in your life where your faith leads the way. It is not always an easy journey. In order to start something new, you have to let go of old things. One thing that helps me with change is to imagine reaching a hand out to God. If I am holding onto something, then there is not enough room for Him to give me anything new. This image reminds me to let everything go – even my son and to hold up empty hands to God. My new start took place right after I recommitted my life to God. This time it was very different. This time it really meant something to me and it brought new hope to my life, finally!

Fortunately, I wasted no time in seeking out a small group in this same church immediately after accepting Christ. The group was made up of a dozen thirty something(s) that were all either single or divorced. Roughly half had never been married and the group was equally male and female. The purpose of the group was not to date each other, but to reach deeper levels of faith and learn about life together through our common circumstances. We were named the "Classics" and this group helped me to start taking inventory of who I was and who I wanted to become. Soon I started to read the Bible more frequently and pursued a spiritually healthier social group. For the first time in my life I could talk openly in a safe environment with no pre-judgments! It didn't matter what the subject was, and even feelings about the loss of my son were not off limits. Life for me was beginning to get much better!

The only person who felt threatened by my attending this new group was the woman I was dating at the time. She was brought up in an environment where her family never really practiced faith. She believed in God, but had never put faith into action or sought out explanations to why people believed the way they did. Suddenly, she could see this huge change in me and did not like the fact that now she had to share me with others who could better relate to the feelings that I was expressing. I eventually ended that relationship and stayed on with the group.

A short time later, I began to date my current wife who also was a member of that same small group. Neither one of us saw it coming, but there was a definite chemistry that became evident one day during a church hayride for singles. This led to one date, then another, and eventually we asked to leave the group, as we were getting more serious about each other and it seemed the right thing to do. After all, it was a <u>singles</u> group. We both felt it was the right decision. Yet we did miss having a group to discuss spiritual matters with.

My wife has been an excellent influence over my spiritual life. She motivates me to dive deeper in the Word and into my heart. I would have never believed that we could actually pray together and talk about our faith with each other: that was definitely uncharted territory! But we actually started praying together long before we were married, which was also new to me and quite a blessing

We eventually were married and moved to a new city where we church shopped for a while and were clearly unsure of what we were really seeking. This was very difficult as now we only had ourselves to look to for spiritual food. It is so important to have several different resources for spiritual food, i.e. the Bible, Church, Small Groups, and Support Groups, etc. Recovery groups were a huge, beneficial step for me and also led to additional support groups like Alanon (for family members of alcoholics), and ACA (Adult Children of Alcoholics). At the time, this was the closest I had come to taking the 4th step of the 12 step recovery program; a character inventory.

We eventually found a church to really connect with and even sought out small groups. When we did not match up with any of the groups available, we decided to start our own group for couples without children, which proved to fill a definite need. We named the group "Kidless Career Couples" which only meant that we were all kidless at that point in time. Years later, we moved out of state and the group dissolved. But many of us still keep in contact to this day and pray regularly for each other.

> **"I knew the second I mentioned anything about my late son, everything would change within the group dynamic"**

This small group was an awesome change for me, as I had struggled in the past with groups. Many times in previous groups the members would spend the first 30 minutes rambling on about their kids. Not only was this uncomfortable for me, but I knew the second I mentioned anything about my late son everything would change within the group dynamic. A complete paradigm shift frequently resulted when people heard my story. People would immediately become uncomfortably quiet as they imagined losing their own child. Nobody ever knew what to say to me after that information was shared which made me even more uncomfortable!

Thank God for this new group where I could speak freely! It was the best thing ever! As a matter-of-fact, our small group model was to eventually split the group off into separate cells, which would then grow into new groups, and so on. Well, our group bonded at such a deep level that we never wanted to split up! We all just kept growing deeper and more transparent with each other. It was richly satisfying.

Probably one of the most significant triumphs in our group was that we learned to pray out loud with each other. While praying out loud sounds very easy, there are usually at least a few individuals within any group that are uncomfortable doing this. The way we overcame this challenge was to list all the prayer requests on 3x5 cards and then pass them around until everyone had a card with 2 or 3 prayers listed, which were not to be their own requests. We then chose someone to open and someone else to close the group prayer, and one-by-one took turns reading the cards which had specific request details listed. This level of detail made it very easy for someone, who was unfamiliar with the requesting party, to simply read the pertinent information. In addition, everyone would take the card home and pray daily for these requests until we met again, where we would update the cards, add new requests, and exchange again. It worked terrifically! We kept a visual list of the answers to our prayers, which was greatly faith-strengthening. It's powerful to repeatedly see God's answers to our prayers!

Fresh Perspective

On an individual level I've found it very helpful to keep a personal journal of all my answered prayers. The Kidless Career Couples group also kept a journal of the prayer requests along with the answers. It's surprising at how fast the answered prayers add up! It is a tangible confirmation of how much God cares for us and a true tribute to Him when we see the power and effectiveness of prayer happening right in front of our own eyes. Our part in this miraculous process is sharing our requests with Him. What a privilege! It became an excellent witness to others, even outside of our group, who would regularly bring more and more prayer requests to our group. Once the word got out, a rush of requests came flooding in; which was a wonderful "problem" for our group to have!

I encourage you to keep a journal of your answered prayer requests. This exercise really can shore-up your faith. Many times, when I am navigating some type of challenge in my life, I remember to review some of the answered prayers listed; and in short order my faith is increased. All of a sudden the challenge seems less difficult as I realize that it *too* shall pass!

Faith Tip:

Seeking out a small group or life group at a local church, surrounding yourself with other Believers, praying and reading your Bible daily can bring healing to your soul.

Simple Truth:

By sharing your story with trusted friends in a safe small group environment, you can release the burden you have been carrying, and can really begin the healing process

Encouraging News!

Memory Verse:

And hope does not disappoint us, because God has poured out his love into our hearts by the Holy Spirit whom He has given us. Romans 5:5 NIV

My Journal:

What does this subject or scripture reading make you think or feel?

_____

_____

_____

_____

_____

_____

_____

_____

_____

_____

_____

_____

_____

_____

_____

_____

_____

_____

_____

Chapter 8

Giving Back and
Helping Others who are Hurting

Helping others is a wonderful way to promote your own healing. When we start paying attention to others we stop thinking about ourselves and it takes the focus off of our pain. Of course, there are some things to keep in mind when offering help to others. We have to be in the right frame of mind in order to be of good use to anyone. Step one is to make sure that your life is in some level of balance and establish good boundaries when managing your time and energy.

Adjacent to the hospital where they performed Bobby's liver transplants, was another hospital that specialized in cancer treatments through the use of bone marrow transplants. Because of the close proximity and our extended time spent at the hospital, we met several other families going through their own severe medical situations. Many times these life and death circumstances compel us to want to help others around us who are also in the same situation. While at first this seems quite normal, it can become overwhelming if we are not careful. For example, instead of just watching the blood-work numbers and details of your own family member, now you have several others to pay attention to and it can really weigh you down. We met so many wonderful people through all of these experiences, some of who are no longer with us here on earth, but still linger in our memories. I would not trade these experiences for anything. Praying for others will lift you up and is the right thing to do. But it is also important to remember that you need to maintain your own strength as well for yourself and your family. So healthy boundaries need to be established for just how much you can add to your own load, without tipping the scales of balance. Be your own judge: your heart will tell you.

> **"I believe that God places us in certain situations with other people where we can provide much needed assistance."**

On the subject of helping others; I believe that God places us in certain situations along with other people where we can provide much needed assistance. There have been numerous times since Bobby's death that I have been able to communicate with other people who were either going through something as severe; or who have already lost a child and are afraid to talk about their experiences and feelings. It gives me a deep sense of honor to help someone who is hurting by simply listening and empathizing. One of the main reasons people keep to themselves is that they assume there are not many who have experienced this sort of trauma in their lives, and it's very difficult to share these deep emotions with someone who can not relate by personal experience. But, I have experienced, on several occasions, God's undeniable plan for me to help someone else who has lost a loved one.

What are the odds that while serving as a Homeowner Associations President which included only twenty homes, two of those families would have recently lost one of their own children? One of the gentlemen was hurting tremendously inside after his son committed suicide with absolutely no warning. The tragedy was that this father did not have anyone in his life that he could relate with to share the consuming thoughts and emotions that he was experiencing daily. He was not even comfortable sharing his feelings with his wife who was hurting in her own way. To make matters worse, he had retired a few years earlier and had very few additional interests or activities to keep him preoccupied. The result on him was that everything bottled up inside until he became angry and depressed himself.

Shortly after I met him, we discovered our mutual experience of loss. Not only did the tears fall, but all the floodgates opened up and he was able to process these deeply buried emotions. I was just along for the ride, so to speak, as once I reached out to him God did the rest. It gave me a wonderful feeling inside to know that he felt comfortable sharing with me on this kind of level, after he had been waiting so long to let go.

The other family in our association had recently experienced a loss of their adult daughter through a natural disaster just weeks before she was to be married. This left the parents feeling completely devastated and wounded. Upon introducing myself to the mother, once again it was not long before we discovered that we had both shared this kind of loss and she began to share her story. This accident was so recent that she was still in the phase of grief where she was questioning how God could let this happen. I shared with her that I settled that question for myself by choosing to believe that God is still in control and He has a plan that is much more than we can ever conceive of with our earthly minds. Actually, it is crucial for our healing to remember that God has a plan for each and every one of us, even after our loss. As I referenced earlier, Jeremiah 29:11 says " For I know the plans I have for you," declares the Lord, "plans to prosper you and not to harm you, plans to give you a hope and a future."

She went on to ask me how I dealt with those seemingly unanswerable questions like the ones that kept nagging at her. I explained the concept of creating a file folder inside my mind titled "To be answered later by God." Whenever I was wrestling with a question or thought in my mind that I could not answer, I would visualize placing it into this folder. This allowed me to stop cycling it through my brain over and over, which brought an immediate sense of much-needed calm and serenity. That way I reminded myself that God was working on issue and I did not have to focus on it anymore. She thought about my answer for a while and began to finally experience a little peace for the first time in a long time. I can remember noticing on her face how comforted she became by just recognizing that she was not the only person in the world who was struggling with this type of loss. The result once again, was that I became the one who was truly blessed by the outcome; because God had shown me how to help someone in need. She was in desperate need for this special validation of her feelings that only someone who walked in her shoes could ever provide.

Even after moving to another state, God continues to regularly connect me with people who have lost their children. Many times in the normal course of business, I will either ask certain questions or provide some background on myself which leads to discovering this commonality. In these moments, God is able to step in and help through me because He knows that I am "at the ready" to share my faith in Jesus and to help others connect with Him when their lives have been in total turmoil! The good news is that God can do this through anyone who is open to helping others.

To my surprise, it is not just for parents losing children, but anyone losing a loved one as well. I have conversed with several people lately that have lost their mother, who also was their best friend. Even though it is not the same type of situation, our God can and does work through anyone who will let Him! I can vividly remember one of these clients asking me "How long after your son died, did you stop crying?" I was amazed by her questions and said, "Do you mean every day?" It brought her great comfort just to know of someone else who has been healed from such a deep wound even though a scar remains. What a privilege it is to have the opportunity to share the awesome power of our God with people in need of His help and healing!

Most recently, a young couple had just lost their daughter during an early forced birth due to complications with infection. The baby girl lived for only two hours. But I was able to meet with them and pray for this family and for their healing from the inevitable grief to follow. During these types of traumatic situations, very few people actually know what to say to comfort the parents. Helping others will strengthen your own healing. I encourage you to work toward helping others in the future after becoming stronger in your faith. There are so many families who need to hear that our God is much bigger than any loss they are feeling and that He alone can restore them!

Fresh Perspective

My hope is for grievers to come along-side other grievers to share God's strength and healing power in their lives! God connects willing souls with others that have lost their loved one, because He knows that the real healing begins when we reach out to help someone else in the midst of our own pain.

As part of your grief recovery, please consider volunteering for some type of organization that you have an interest in or a passion for. Once you get involved you may be surprised by the healing that starts in your own life! One other benefit is that we really do not have to look very far to find someone who has a harder situation to navigate through than our own. This shift in perspective can be a positive influence in our own grief recovery.

Simple Truth:

God is working through me in the lives of others.

Faith Tip:

By helping others in the middle of their difficulties, not only does it take our attention off ourselves, but it can also provide peace and healing through practicing gratitude.

Encouraging News!

Memory Verse:

The Lord is good, a refuge in times of trouble. He cares for those who trust in Him. Nahum 1:7 NIV

My Journal:

What does this subject or scripture reading make you think or feel?

_____

_____

_____

_____

_____

_____

_____

_____

_____

_____

_____

_____

_____

_____

_____

_____

_____

_____

Chapter 9

Acts of Remembrance

Part of the loss we feel inside is the fear of losing the memories we had with our loved one. Sometimes we can experience the feeling of missing out on the future plans we had already imagined; or we simply miss our loved ones presence.

Thankfully, there can be many ways to stay connected to the memories we have of our loved ones. I call these "Acts of Remembrance." This can be a healthy part of the recovery process in moderation of course. The key is to discover which type of act of remembrance works for you. Everyone is different and each griever has their own personal memories that are dear to them. Some of the acts that work for me are listed below. But please remember that this subject is a very personal one between you and your loved one. So create some traditions, acts, or tributes that work for you.

Birthday Celebrations

There were several times during his frequent hospital stays that Bobby had to learn to eat and digest solid foods all over again. Through all of these events, he never forgot his passion for McDonald's cheeseburger and fries! We used to take turns feeding him small pieces of the burger and watching his smile grow large! And, boy would he reach for the fries! But then again, who doesn't love McDonald's fries? Another bonus was the opportunity to support the Ronald McDonald House Charities, as we knew first hand how they helped families like ours! So, every year I celebrate Bobby's birthday by first getting a "Happy Birthday"

balloon, preferably with Mickey Mouse on it. Secondly, I pick up his all-time favorite meal; a McDonald's cheeseburger and fries!

Then, I proceed to a quite place outdoors like a stream (Minnehaha Falls, Minnesota), or arboretum (in Minnesota), a golf course in the mountains (in Korea), a rock ledge (in Missouri), by the ocean (in Florida), and on the top of a mountain (in Arizona) just to name a few. I also bring along some of his pictures, books, and a few of his toys that I have kept through the years (sometimes I can remember so vividly the two of us playing with these toys together).

I also bring along a CD of Kenny G's titled "Silhouette" which was the music I listened to on the way to the hospital when we spent our last day together.

Later I realized that even the song titles seemed to relate to Bobby's story (Against Doctors Orders, Saving the Best for Last, Pastel, Let Go, and Going Home)! *During the first year or two after Bobby died, there were many times that I would drive along some country road with the windows down and these songs blasting loud enough so he and I could share them together. It may sound off the wall, but it sure brought me some comfort, as it felt like he was right there with me. A few years later I won tickets to see Kenny G live in concert. It was such a moving experience that I felt my emotions take over and sobbed with abandon! Rivers of tears are key to cleansing the soul of the pain of such loss – even for men. I thanked God for this uniquely healing opportunity.*

Back to lunch… What I do is listen to the music, review the book and pictures and share lunch "with Bobby," all the time remembering how big his smile would be when reaching for another fry! Then I write him a letter, usually on a tear-stained napkin and thank him for how much I have learned from him; how much I am grateful that God entrusted him to me even for a short time; and for using this experience to lead me to Christ! Then, I attach the letter to the Birthday balloon and set it free while imagining that he eventually receives it in his little hands in Heaven…

> *"It is very important for any bereaved parent*
> *to find some type of their own tribute*
> *for their child, whatever form that takes."*

Every time I finish this tribute, I feel so much closer to Bobby and to God. I believe that it is very important for any bereaved parent to find some type of their own tribute for their child, whatever form that takes. The emotional release and subsequent relief are tremendously important in dealing with the feelings of loss.

Bobby's Homecoming

On the anniversary of the day Bobby went home to be with the Lord (September 25th), I also perform a tribute to him and his life by celebrating the same way as his Birthday mentioned earlier, only skipping the Birthday balloon. I often wonder if he now has 2 birthdays – one on earth, and one in Heaven.

Bobby's Candle

After Bobby went home to be with Jesus, we were left with all the reminders around us like toys, pictures, clothes, and even more toys. It was painful to see the toys, but no Bobby. After a few weeks, we decided to pack up some of the most important keepsake items in a trunk and set aside the remaining items for a yard sale. Yet even after some time had passed, a yard sale still would have been way too difficult for us. So our best friends stepped up and took care of everything. The proceeds were deposited into his donation account and later given to the hospital for liver transplantation research along with the donated money from the funeral.

We took one of our favorite 8x10 pictures of Bobby with my Army camouflage uniform shirts on and placed it in a frame on a corner table in the living room. We kept a lit candle there with his picture for the first few days, and then decided it was much safer to replace the candle with a lamp. Needless to say, we went through several replacement light bulbs.

I tried many things to remain close to Bobby and cling to the happy feelings so I could treasure them a little longer. It was so very hard to let go and fill this huge void in my life. And to some this gesture may seem small. But whenever I saw his picture and that glowing light it kept a special feeling alive in my heart. Sometimes it's the little things that seem to bring us the most comfort. I will always remember how my heart would skip a beat when that lamp would burn out another bulb! I could not change it fast enough! This tribute meant so much to me, and it seemed like all I had left. It was like the feeling I had at the grave site, after his body was laid beneath the soil. I felt very concerned that Bobby would become cold and I wanted so much to give him another blanket or just hold him tightly to my chest again. Then I could keep him safe and warm. I had to let go. But how could I?

We even added keepsakes in his casket which included his favorite Mickey Mouse watch, and his "good luck" elephant given by some friends in Japan. There seems to be no place for logic or rationale, when it comes to parental urges and desires that are buried deep inside. The truth is, who really cares how anyone else thinks at this point? It's how we think and feel that really matters anyway!

Fresh Perspective

Even these many years later, I still find ways to celebrate the life and memories of my son. My biggest fear is that with the passing of time these memories will fade. That is why I make the time consistently year after year to recall and savor our cherished times together. Yet I contain these acts of remembrance within pre-determined days. And I limit them to about 2 days per year so my perspective remains healthy and balanced. Grievers must not permit themselves to become stuck in unending or constant mourning. We <u>must</u> move on, to each new day.

Understanding that there may continue to be several triggers that happen regularly, as time passes they will become less frequent and less severe. On the other hand, an act of remembrance is deliberately practiced in an effort to remember joyful times together with our loved one. This is the primary reason for establishing some boundaries for the frequency of these times so we can stay balanced in our grief recovery.

For your own healing, please take some time to discover some type of tribute that works for you so you can delight in the joyful memories with your loved one, while embracing each new day God gives you.

Simple Truth:

Recounting good memories in a balanced amount/way can provide comfort and promote healing.

Faith Tip:

It can be important to some people in their healing process to determine a healthy way of remembering those who were important and provide hope that they will be reunited some day.

Encouraging News!

Memory Verse:

My comfort in my suffering is this: Your promise preserves my life. Psalm 119:50 NIV

My Journal:

What does this subject or scripture reading make you think or feel?

_____

_____

_____

_____

_____

_____

_____

_____

_____

_____

_____

_____

_____

_____

_____

_____

_____

_____

_____

_____

_____

_____

Chapter 10

Unanswered Questions are OKAY

When we endure such a horrible loss, questions can bombard our mind. Why; what if; how could God permit this; what did I do to deserve this; and on, and on. We don't have to have all the answers right now... and that's okay. The truth is that nobody on earth has the answers. The most important thing to do is to trust our faith and remember that God is the *only* one with the answers to our questions. Sometimes He tells us the answers. Sometime He asks us to wait and trust that He is good, despite our pain. If you are struggling with searching for answers that seem to be eluding you, always remember that you are not alone. Others have been where you are right now.

When I was faced with many unanswered questions and my mind would start swimming in confusion, I would recall the file folder which I imagined in my mind named "To be answered later by God." Then I took those unanswered questions that had been bothering me and drop them into that folder. I have gained a lot of peace by practicing this technique. For me, it means that I can finally put to rest the questions that keep rolling through my mind, over, and over, and over again. Not only do I find an immediate benefit; but after pondering the relevance of these questions sometime later, I have determined that when I do arrive in Heaven, I probably will not even care about the answers anymore! When all things are revealed by the Father, earthly questions will resolve and our thoughts will no longer be limited as they are here.

> *"The truth is that God has infinite control of everything including time, and He is not limited by the boundaries of time progressing in the manner that we comprehend."*

It is interesting to me that only through the passing of time have I grown enough in my faith to recognize some of the "why's" that have been answered. It seems that when we are in the midst of trauma, our minds cannot even conceive of any logical explanation. Well… perhaps there was really nothing logical about it in the first place. As humans, we like to think along this logical timeline that tends to make sense and keep an order to events. The truth is that God has infinite control of everything including time, and He is not limited by the boundaries of time progressing in the manner that we comprehend.

Recently, I had a picture in my mind that illustrated God taking events from different periods of time and moving them around in a sequence that made sense only to Him in order to accomplish His goals and plans.

Who are we to assume that our minds can even comprehend what the Creator of the universe is working out in all of our lives? I for one am relieved that it is impossible to think on that level. A child-like faith works well for me. By design we were not created to think on that level.

There is peace in *not* having control and in simply trusting that if it is really important, God will reveal *His* thoughts to us in ways *we* can understand. This has been written over and over again in the scriptures as referring to thinking and acting as children. In all honesty, I have been able to discover only two things that we really have control over and they are 1) how we think and react to things and 2) how we treat other people. God ultimately controls everything else.

As I am writing this chapter, my sister is dying of cancer and will probably be going home to be with the Lord in the next few days. My sister and her children are all Believers in Jesus and have a strong faith. But even with a strong faith, the children are questioning God's plan for their mother. While witnessing this, I mentioned to them that regardless of what happens, they must remember that God has His own beautiful plans for their mother and her life belongs to <u>Him</u>. If He brings her home, then her work here on earth is complete. But her life in Heaven is only just beginning.

> *"At these times it is very important to cling to hope and look at life through eyes of faith."*

When God does bring her home, we should not get mad at Him because He gave her life in the first place. And it is God's right alone to determine when to move her from earth to Heaven. At these times it is very important to cling to hope and look at life through eyes of faith. When we look at things this way, God can instill His peace inside us, which provides the much needed comfort to endure even the hardest of times.

Many times people will act like they have all of the answers and throw around a cliché or two. The problem with this is that they are hollow thoughts and can be very trite. I remember resenting those little quips that people tried to comfort me with. When people said things like "God doesn't give you anything you can't handle," I felt like replying that I wish I wasn't that strong, so this wouldn't have happened to me! Oh sure, they meant well. But the truth is that everyone would have been better off if we just simply acted like compassionate people and supportively grieved along side our loved ones. And just be there for them without suggesting any answers at all.

The Three Births

Someone once explained that there are three births in our lives. The first is when we are born into the world. We find ourselves very comfortable in our mother's womb, where we are warm and nourished. Then suddenly we die to that life and are born into a very cold, bright and noisy world. We learn to adapt and get comfortable in this new world. Then the second birth occurs when we discover and accept Jesus Christ as our Lord and Savior. We are fed, guided and comforted by our Heavenly Father. And finally, when our journey on this earth ends, we are born into our new lives in Heaven. In this third birth, we receive new bodies and are reunited with those who have gone before us. What a beautiful and comforting truth!

To summarize, I believe that even though we all strive to answer the most difficult questions, some are better off remaining unanswered for now. This way our faith and hope can be strengthened and we in turn will be stronger for it. ***You see, it is impossible for our faith to be strengthened if it is not stretched by being tested.***

Fresh Perspective

It is during difficult times of testing that our faith is renewed and blossoms into a whole new level. Our faith begins to build on itself and we become stronger with each test. That does not mean that circumstances will get any easier, just that we become better equipped to handle each challenge. In essence, faith begets more faith as we progress through each challenge towards the triumph which is ours with God's help.

One key is to remember how much our faith has grown, and then recognize that we will overcome this new challenge too. Sometimes, by keeping a journal we can review previous challenges that were overcome by faith, and this can provide the confidence we need to keep enduring and pressing through to victory!

Simple Truth:

Our faith is strengthened by passing through the tests in life, both the good and the painful.

Faith Tip:

This side of Heaven we may never understand, But we can trust the heart of our caring, loving, and compassionate God and know we're always in His hands.

Encouraging News!

Memory Verse:

We live by faith and not by sight.
2 Corinthians 5:7 NIV

My Journal:

What does this subject or scripture reading make you think or feel?

---

* PART THREE *

A New Hope-Filled Future

Chapter 11

Healing Our Spirit

Get alone with The Word.

There is absolutely no substitute for taking time alone each day, perhaps even several times a day, to review scripture or just talk with God. Remember, *it's about the relationship, not a religious ritual.*

When I mention the word "alone" the truth is God is always with us – especially during the times when we feel the most alone, left out, or forgotten. It seems that when we feel alone, our minds can be an open doorway for depression to sneak in and undermine our faith. The way to fight and win against depression comes by getting completely alone with God on a regular basis which permits hope to replace hurt, depression, and loneliness and eventually leads to healing.

It takes consistency to facilitate true healing because our minds are constantly doing battle with all kinds of thoughts – some good, and some not-so-good. This battle of the mind is monumental in healing through grief recovery, and it must be fought daily. Understand also that the world (through the devil) will try to work against us in our healing by trying to convince us that we should not or cannot feel joy, peace, or happiness again. That is a big lie!

Our God is so much larger, than any lie that has ever been spoken and there is no situation too difficult for Him to bring healing! But you have to believe it through your eyes of faith.

> *"Our God is so much larger than any lie that has ever been spoken and there is no situation too difficult for Him to bring healing! But you have to believe it through your eyes of faith."*

Recently, I realized something that revolutionized my thinking. You see, many times you hear people say things like "God is here with me," or "God is going with us." Even while those statements are true, please understand that God is already everywhere at all times and we can choose whether or not to engage with Him and feel His presence. Think about it, God, The Creator and Sustainer of the universe, has promised to be <u>with</u> you, to <u>care</u> for you and <u>heal</u> you – if you nourish a relationship with Him. When I meditated on this idea for a while, it made sense to me that God is so much bigger than someone you take along with you – He is already everywhere at all times! This idea also helps make sense of multiple people connecting with God simultaneously, it's completely possible! So you see, you are never alone…period!

There is another very important item to consider pertaining to the feeling of loneliness, and it comes long after the funeral for our loved ones. It takes place after everyone has left and the dust settles. There, in the blink of an eye, everything becomes quiet, friends and family have returned to their own lives and now it is time to face the emptiness.

> *"When I have reached out to others who are hurting, it often heals me."*

So many times at this point the hurting person turns inward, and over time it becomes harder to reach out to others. Those who have not lost a loved one close to them just don't know what to do or how to help. So, openly let them know that it is paramount for family, friends, and co-workers to stay engaged and in-touch with you regularly. Ask them to plan and schedule times in the future to make periodic phone calls, visits, or even to invite you out somewhere. Hurting people need to know that others are still available for them to spend time with – even if it is just to listen.

Something I have discovered in my own life is that when I have reached out to others who are hurting, it often heals me in many ways. I believe it has a lot to do with how God has wired each of us at our very core. He placed inside of us a desire to help each other with an unselfish heart; and this is why it feels so good when we help someone and expect nothing in return. This truth becomes evident when we witness some type of incident or serious accident. People tend to jump right in and help regardless of who is at fault, the color of their skin, gender, or nationality. The truth is we feel compelled when something like this happens. God has woven this into the very fabric of our being – what an awesome thing for Him to do for us!

Daily Prayers, Scripture Readings, and Declarations

My daily prayer life has changed for the better much more that words can describe. It has been said that your attitude is everything and I really believe this to be true. To this point, I believe that our spirit is most vulnerable to attacks first thing in the morning when we wake up. Therefore, my wife and I started a practice of reciting this scripture verse together before our feet touch the floor; "This is the day that the Lord has made, I will rejoice and be glad in it! (*Psalm 118:24*) – Something GREAT is going to happen for us today! – We get to do something for Jesus today!" I can't tell you how much this single act has improved my attitude.

The next important step in my morning routine is to pray in the same quiet place every day where I can be alone with the Father. Also, I imagine Jesus sitting on the bed, holding my hand while I am praying. Once I started visualizing His face and His hand, it really made me feel His presence like nothing ever has before. There is something special that happens when you really feel alone with God, and feel that holy connectedness that cannot come from anyone else.

Another suggestion is to consider reciting declarations out loud every day. As part of my daily time with God every morning I start by giving God honor, praise, and admiration: asking for and accepting His forgiveness; and then making my requests with adoration and thanksgiving. After I close my prayers, I declare the blessings listed below over myself and my wife; and finally end by reciting scriptures which help me to set my mind straight for the day.

Daily Declarations

* I am a VICTOR not a Victim
* I am God's precious child
* I am the HEAD and not the tail
* I am being PROMOTED
* I am TALENTED and GIFTED
* I am BLESSED and not cursed
* I am HANDSOME and ATTRACTIVE
* I have read the last page (of the Bible) and WE WIN
* I am PROSPEROUS
* God is PLEASED with me
* I have DIVINE PROTECTION
* I come from an AWESOME BLOODLINE (Abraham's descendants)
* I am a THOROUGHBRED
* I am CREATED
* I am HEALTHY
* I have SUPERNATURAL STRENGTH
* I have a BRIGHT FUTURE
* I am a child of the MOST HIGH GOD
* I am WISE, COMPATIONATE, and KIND
* People LIKE me
* I am FORGIVEN
* I am a FRIEND of God
* I am VALUABLE to God
* God is PROSPERING me

* I am FUN to be around
* I have a FUN PERSONALITY
* I am ANOINTED
* I have the PEACE of God
* I am APPROVED
* I have the FAVOR of God
* I have been CHOSEN
* I am going to RISE to new heights
* I am STRONG
* God is on MY side
* I am EXCITED about this day, and I choose to be HAPPY
* I am an OVERCOMER
* I CAN DO what I need to do
* I am more than a CONQUEROR
* I am and have been a BLESSING to others
* Everything I put my hand to will SUCCEED
* I will LEND and not borrow
* I can do all things through CHRIST who gives me the STRENGTH
* I am well able to fulfill my DESTINY
* GOOD THINGS are in store for me
* God has placed inside of me everything I need to live in VICTORY
* God LOVES me
* I am the APPLE of God's eye
* God has filled me with His CREATIVENESS and granted me all the POWER and STRENGTH to overcome any challenge in my life

Scriptures Readings

* In the morning I lay my requests before you and wait in expectation (Psalm 5:3 NIV)
* But seek first His kingdom and His righteousness and all things will be given to you as well (Mathew 6:33) NIV
* But I tell you who hear me, love your enemies, do good to those who hate you (Luke 6:27) NIV

* Oh that You would bless me and enlarge my territory let your hand be with me and keep me from harm (1 Chronicles 4:10) NIV
* If the Lord delights in a man's way, He makes his steps firm, though he stumble, he will not fall, for the Lord upholds him with His hand (Psalm 37:23) NIV
* Do not conform any longer to the patters of this world, but be transformed by the renewing of your mind, Then you will be able to test His good, pleasing, and perfect will (Romans 12:2) NIV
* Trust in the Lord with all your heart and lean not on your own understanding, in all your ways acknowledge Him and He will direct your path (Proverbs 3:5) NIV
* Finally, be strong in the Lord and in His mighty power, put on the full armor of God so you can take your stand against the Devil's schemes (Ephesians 6:10-13) NIV
* For those who hope in the Lord will renew their strength, they will soar high with wings like eagles, they will run and not grow weary, they will walk and not faint (Isaiah 40:31) NIV
* Dear friends let us love one another, for love comes from God, everyone who loves has been born of God and knows God (1 John 4:7) NIV
* Everything in the Heaven and earth are Yours O' Lord, and this is Your kingdom. We adore You as being in control of everything. Riches and honor come from You alone, and You are ruler of all mankind. Your hand controls power and might, and it's at Your discretion that men are made great and given strength (1 Chronicles 29:11) NIV
* Lord you are good and Your mercies endureth forever (1 Chronicles 16:34) NKJV
* Behold, I am the Lord God of all flesh, is their anything too hard for Me? (Jeremiah 32:27) NKJV
* Curds and honey shall he eat that he knows to refuse evil and choose the good. (Isaiah 7:15) NKJV
* Therefore, whether you eat or drink, or whatever you do, do everything to the glory of God (1 Corinthians 10:31) NKJV
* In everything, do to others as you would have them to do to you, for this is the law of the Prophets. (Mathew 7:12) NIV
* "For I tell you the truth, if you have faith the size of a mustard seed you can tell this mountain to move from here to there and

it will obey, nothing will be impossible for you.
(Mathew 17:20) NKJV
* I can do all things through Christ who gives me the strength
(Philippians 4:13) NKJV
* Commit to the Lord whatever I do and my plans will succeed
(Psalm 37:5) NKJV
* Be still, wait patiently for Him, do not fret (Psalm 37:7) NKJV
* Lord, when I am afraid, I will put my trust in you
(Psalm 56:3) NIV
* I submit myself to God, resist the devil and he must flee
(James 4:7-8) NIV
* Set your minds on things above, not on earthly things
(Colossians 3:2) NKJV
* As a man thinks in his heart, so is he. (Proverbs 23:7) NKJV
* My determined purpose is to know Him and the power of His
resurrection! (Philippians 3:10) AMP

Fresh Perspective

Now that I have memorized these scriptures and speak them out
loud daily, I feel much more empowered to do the work that God
has in store for me to do. There are many opportunities throughout
each day to put these scriptures into practice; and scripture is our
weapon to fight and win the battles we face!

The key to empowerment in your daily life is to recall the truth
found in the scriptures. Indeed, it can be difficult for some people
to memorize scripture. It was for me. But when we practice over
and over, before long it becomes embedded in our minds and we
can recall it when we need it. It has begun to payoff exponentially
in my life and I know it can in yours also!

Simple Truth:

Get alone with God and He will provide everything you need to heal and be restored.

Faith Tip:

Speak declarations and scripture verses <u>out-loud</u> daily during your prayer time.

Encouraging News!

Memory Verse:

I can do all things through Christ who gives me the strength. (Philippians 4:13) NIV

My Journal:

What does this subject or scripture reading make you think or feel?

_____

_____

_____

_____

_____

_____

_____

_____

_____

_____

_____

_____

_____

_____

_____

_____

_____

_____

_____

Chapter 12

Miracles Happen

The truth is that there **_are_** such things as miracles and they **_are_** happening around us every day! One of our goals should be to look for and identify them in our daily lives. Recognizing miracles helps us to stay inspired and engaged in life by connecting with our Creator, who after all is the author of these miracles.

Miracles are an important part of the fabric that is woven by God alone and we usually only recognize them upon reflection at a later time. In my own life I have recognized many miracles, and still discover new ones regularly. My faith is not built on miracles, but they help increase my awareness that God is in complete control of my life and that He wants <u>good</u> things for me.

Once you start asking questions, you will be pleasantly surprised to discover that many people around you already have witnessed miracles several times in their own lives. When we open our minds to the possibility of events that cannot be explained, we can see our Creator's fingerprints revealed before our very eyes.

One Seat Left!

Immediately after it was discovered that there was something seriously wrong with our son's health, we took him to an internal medicine specialist who required a biopsy of his liver. Basically, we were trying to find out what was causing his liver function numbers to be abnormal and determine how much, if any, of his liver was not functioning. During this procedure, my military unit was being deployed to Honduras, Central America. While we were awaiting liver biopsy results, there was really nothing else we could do during that time. We did not yet know how seriously ill he really was. My heart was torn; do I deploy with my unit and the soldiers who I have been training? Or, do I stay here and support my family? After discussing it with my family and consulting with my Superior (First Sergeant), we decided that I would deploy with my unit under a personal promise by my First Sergeant that he would get me home if it was determined that a transplant was required, even if he had to pay for a flight himself! I knew he was a man of integrity, so I agreed.

Each day during the deployment I would call my previous wife (Bobby's mother) via military short-wave radio and civilian phone operators to check on the biopsy results. I remember having this feeling of unrest and a constant knot in my stomach while trying to focus on my work. Sure enough, one week into the mission we discovered that our son had severe liver scerocis and would require a transplant. When that call came, my heart sank as our worst fears were becoming reality!

As agreed, my First Sergeant and I jumped into a truck and headed through the mountains to the military airport about 5 hours away. Upon arriving, we inquired about the next flight out to the United States. We were informed that we had just missed the last flight out for the next three days, and that very plane was on the airstrip preparing for takeoff! After hearing this, my First Sergeant became visibly upset and disappeared for a few minutes. Somehow, during that time he managed to contact the Airbase Commander and get the brakes put on that plane! This was completely unheard of and was a miracle in itself!

Instantly I was rushed through customs and into a jeep that took me across the airfield to the C5A cargo plane which was powering up on the runway for takeoff. Now, this type of aircraft carried mostly cargo and is one of the largest planes in our military. There was only a small section reserved for passenger seating and when I arrived on the plane I discovered that there was only one seat remaining! Making this event even more incredible was that this seat just happened to be next to the very physician who delivered my son! He was originally from Panama and had volunteered to help some of their local hospitals during a politically difficult time in his home country. But the miracles do not stop there. After we took off I brought him up to date on everything, and of course he was full of questions. It was an incredible relief and greatly comforting to have someone to talk to who not only understood, but who I already knew and trusted. He was just the person I needed to talk to at that moment. You could say that he was just what the doctor ordered! After catching him up on everything, I inquired how he was getting back to the base located in Georgia, as we were arriving in South Carolina. He said that he planned to stay the night and catch another flight out in the morning. I mentioned to him that one of my soldiers had volunteered for the drive to pick me up and I would gladly drop him off at his house by the base. He graciously agreed, and later when we arrived in town I asked where he lived, only to discover that he had been my neighbor all along. His house was one street away from mine. I hadn't even known! God sure works in mysterious ways indeed!

This encounter, along with the sequence of events that had transpired gave me great confidence that God was indeed in control. I reconciled to myself that there was absolutely no way that any of these events were coincidental. There were too many for that to be the case. Immediately, I could feel a peace within myself that somehow everything was going to be okay, because God was in the driver's seat!

Protection from the Storm!

Years later, my current wife and I moved to Florida. Only two weeks after our move hurricane Charlie ripped through our new town destroying most of the county. The eye of the storm passed over our new home that we had not even closed on yet. We had no idea where to evacuate to. So we headed north until the weather reports became clearer. The Lord kept us safe as we drove to the opposite side of the state and completely missed the storm.

In the aftermath we drove back to check on our new home. There was complete devastation all around us. We expected the worst. But when we arrived we were amazed to see that our home was completely untouched and safe! We were able to eventually close on the sale of our home and in the meantime begin helping everyone in the town around us dig out from the rubble and rebuild their homes. The property we were renting was safe as well and actually had power, which allowed us to charge our tools every evening for use during the following day in boarding up damaged homes for protection. God directed and protected us!

God has performed miracle after miracle in my life. As I reflect back over my life, I can see time after time that He was making these divine connections happen. I often wonder if God smiles when we finally figure them out and give Him the credit!

For additional stories also see the "Feather story and Voicemail from Heaven in chapter 14."

> **"Fault looks back, Fear looks around, and Faith looks up."**

Far too often we go through life with our heads down, only focusing on the path immediately in front of us. The truth is that when we lift our heads up and focus on the bigger picture, we discover that God loves each of us as His own precious child. When we really understand this we treat others as valued and our lives can become a vibrant reflection of His love. To further illustrate this point, I once heard an expression that says "Fault looks back, Fear looks around, and Faith looks up." Where are you looking?

Fresh Perspective

Begin to look for miracles that God has done or is doing in your own life right now. Some are small and may only seem like coincidence. I challenge you to look deeper: because the natural cannot always explain the supernatural. You can take comfort in knowing that your Supernatural God is with you in the midst of your grief and is the source of your healing. Miracles are God's way of reminding us that He is in complete control, and that He loves and cares for each one of us as His precious children!

Please make it your goal to keep your head up and your eyes fixed firmly on heaven. No matter how you are feeling or how difficult your situation is, I promise to you that God will work in your life in a big way and you will never want to look down again!

Simple Truth:

Miracles are happening all around us,
Can you see them?

Faith Tip:

God is always at work in your life and He smiles
when you turn your eyes toward Him.

Encouraging News!

Memory Verse:

Set your minds on things above, not on
earthly things.   (Colossians 3:2) NIV

My Journal:

What does this subject or scripture reading make you think or feel?

_____

_____

_____

_____

_____

_____

_____

_____

_____

_____

_____

_____

_____

_____

_____

_____

_____

_____

Chapter 13

Holidays

Looking back, some of my most difficult times have been in dealing with the feelings of loss during holidays, birthdays and other special days. With each passing year, it becomes a little easier for the most part. Yet I do not remember with longing that feeling of being "whole" as a family, and the joy that was shared. When I notice other families interacting the way that I used to with mine, it has been particularly difficult. It usually brings back terrific memories, followed by a deep sense of loss… even now, many years later.

When I think back to the first few years after my son went to be with the Lord, I can remember becoming so overwhelmed at a church Christmas play that I could not handle all the feelings bombarding me and had to quickly leave. I felt such a rush of emotions, and the feelings were very intense and gut-wrenching. Even though my family was there, they had no clue how to console me, what to say or what I needed.

Other difficult times were when people were gushing over pictures of their children or grandchildren. I usually just replied with something like "you must be so proud or, how cute, etc." when inside, my heart was writhing in pain and thinking, "if they only knew." But I avoided telling them because it would squelch their joy if they found out. It becomes a real quandary when you outlive your child. Most people are not sure what to say or how to act, which creates few opportunities to share your life-experiences with anyone. Losing a child is a parent's greatest fear. It is a fortunate thing that not all parents have to face this kind of loss.

In chapter 9 you may recall some of the traditions that I have adopted as a way of remembering my son and acknowledging my feelings in a healthy way. Let me encourage you to find what works best for you. Personally, I think it is much healthier to practice some traditions which give you permission to grieve the loss and remember the special memories, than it is to ignore your memories and feelings. If you deny yourself the opportunity to feel these emotions, you can cause undue hardship on yourself and delay your healing.

It is also very important to establish some healthy guidelines for grief and time for initial periods of intense mourning. Give yourself permission to let it all flow freely, but for a pre-determined period of time. The Bible establishes a period of "weeping and mourning." Ancient laws prescribe 40 days for mourning according to Genesis 50:3 and 30 days according to Deuteronomy 34:8. This can be a guideline for you; as it has been a proven approach throughout the ages. That may not seem realistic to some people. But the message I believe is to give yourself a chance to let it all out, and then start the process of healing. Once you've gone through initial intense mourning, it's important to restrain future periods of mourning and remembrance to shorter timeframes. Please review Chapter 9 for helpful insight.

The important point to remember is for grievers not to permit themselves to become stuck in never-ending mourning. We must move on to each new day. Always do whatever feels right to you, with the ultimate goal of moving from mourning to healing

> *"Please do not forget that God sacrificed His only Son and knows exactly how you are feeling and how to help you."*

There have been many times that I wished I knew someone who had lost their only child as I did so I could share this grief and sadness with someone who could really understand and sympathize. Thank God that He does. It is to Him that I pour out all of my thoughts, and all of my grief and sadness. And, it's through His Word and His touch that I gain comfort and healing. I know He hears me and sees every tear (and there have been many). Remember, God sacrificed His only Son and knows exactly how you are feeling and just how to help you.

With the passing of time I have become stronger in my faith and more willing to share my story with people who have not lost a child, without fear of their reactions. For so long I kept it all inside because I felt it would hurt them by taking them to a place in their mind where it would be frightening for them to go. Denying this part of my life's story hurt me deeply. It was similar to the feeling I had during my son's funeral; where I was trying to keep my tears inside as a "good and strong" man would do and then thinking to myself at grave-side, "what a bunch of crap! I am going to let this out regardless of what anyone else thinks!" It sure felt much better than holding it in! Now, I am not afraid to share my story with anyone, at the appropriate time of course.

Upon considering which holidays are most difficult, I think for me that Birthdays and the day my son died have been the hardest, followed by Christmas. Probably the most confusing of all holidays for me is Father's Day as described below.

Father's Day

Father's Day for me always poses an interesting dilemma. I am a father, that's true. But I no longer receive the traditional Father's Day gifts or recognition. I look around and see other families enjoying themselves and treating dad to a day filled with admiration and appreciation. But for me…I have not yet figured out how to think about this. Please don't get me wrong. I really don't want a "pity party," and remain very grateful that my son is with Jesus.

One very enjoyable thing I did on Father's Day was to wish a "Happy Father's Day" to God in my morning prayers. It was great to recognize God as my Father on this day of celebration! He really has made up for childhood shortages of approval and affection in my life.

Now that several years have passed since my son went to be with the Lord, Father's Day has become less of a gut-wrenching experience for me. In earlier years I felt sad and robbed in some ways. It wasn't an entitlement feeling as much as a feeling of missing out on something special.

For many years I held on to a key chain that my son gave me which read "#1 Dad!" I cherished it so much that when it finally broke I felt terrible, as there was no way of replacing it or the memory. To this day, I still have the key ring itself, which is all that remains: and I keep it with me. I think that trinkets like this can go way beyond being sentimental and many times can trigger deep memories worth recounting.

Once the opportunities for new memories cease, the existing memories become vitally important. Even memories of facial expressions or other details that usually go unnoticed become clearer. It's like replaying the experience to identify something new that perhaps was not noticed before, in an effort to make it a new experience to treasure and appreciate. Some of these thoughts have come to me during the Christmas season as well; I think mostly because they are the toughest times to push through. Fortunately Father's Day is only, after all, one day instead of an entire season.

Another interesting dilemma concerns having a new spouse enter the picture. How do they, or should they, react to your loss or celebration on holidays, etc? My wife is the birth mother of a daughter she gave up for adoption; her only child. I make sure to recognize her on Mother's Day every year. In my opinion, she is still a mother who deserves recognition even though her daughter lives apart from us. I believe that giving her daughter up was a very loving and caring thing to do. She loved her that much and was not selfish like so many others are, even when they know they cannot provide for their new baby.

When you reverse the situation, it can become very difficult for either one or both. Do we celebrate or not? Are there good feelings or sad feelings? What are the answers? The truth is, nobody really knows. And I am inclined to suggest that these feelings are forever changing for each person from day to day, year to year; and require sensitive communication prior to major events or holidays to gauge how the other is feeling.

Even years later, there are times my mind becomes flooded by several memories all at the same time. It usually brings me to tears, which has been a great release that I am no longer afraid of. Thank God He has given me a tender heart! Please keep in mind that letting your feelings out will help you in your healing process. It has for me and it can for you too.

Fresh Perspective

Sometimes you may feel like hiding from a holiday or just ignoring it. Remember that there are things you can do to soften the feelings during these days. Take it easy on yourself and try to recognize that you may have extra sensitivity during different holidays – it's okay.

You may want to limit the number of holiday parties or events that you attend. Also, always remember that you have permission to leave any situation that feels too uncomfortable or brings up overwhelming. Your hosts will understand if they know that you are grieving a loss, and will usually do everything they can to support you.

Throughout the years during the holidays, I have been able to feel God's presence and know that He is here with me. I take comfort in His plan for me and my life, knowing that I can trust my future to Him! Plus, I know with confidence that my son and I will be re-united someday and in the meantime he will not feel any more pain. Every day he experiences joy to the fullest with the Savior of the world - and that brings me the greatest comfort of all!

Simple Truth:

*God will hold you and comfort you like nobody
else can – Trust Him.*

Faith Tip:

*Finding some new ways of celebrating holidays
can be helpful, possibly even traveling to different
destinations – try something new!*

Encouraging News!

Memory Verse:

*Praise be to the God and Father of our Lord
Jesus Christ, the Father of compassion and the God
of all comfort, who comforts us in all our troubles,
so that we can comfort those in any trouble with the
comfort we ourselves have received from God.
(2 Corinthians 1:3-4) NIV*

My Journal:

What does this subject or scripture reading make you think or feel?

_____

_____

_____

_____

_____

_____

_____

_____

_____

_____

_____

_____

_____

_____

_____

_____

_____

_____

Chapter 14

Inspiring Hope

Feather Story

This is a true story of how God revealed His presence to me. In the funeral home after leaving the private viewing room where all the immediate family had gathered to say their final goodbye to my son, I remember looking to the heavens and asking God through my agony and tears for some kind of sign that my little boy was with Him and that he was okay. Just then, I noticed a bird's feather floating down from the sky right in front of me! I looked around and saw no birds, power lines, or even trees for that matter. I asked myself where this feather could have come from, and by this time the feather was right out in front of me. I did not have to reach for it, I simply held out my hand with my palm facing upward and the feather gently landed squarely in my hand! Perhaps some could explain this event away. But to me it was an immediate and timely answer to my desperate request. I took the feather home with me and placed it in a framed picture of my son. Whenever I passed by, it gave me much needed comfort by reminding me that God answered my prayer.

If that wasn't enough, a little over a year later, when I was stationed in Korea, it happened again! It was the anniversary of my son's death, and I was feeling very alone and sad. With no family around and living in a foreign country, it was especially tough that day. I had taken the day off and was prayer-walking around the military base. I was in a wide-open space in a park which was formerly a golf course and again was asking God for comfort in my grief. Just then, from out of the sky… another feather was drifting down in front of me! Once again, I looked around and did not see any sign of birds or trees within several hundred yards. Then my attention returned to the feather, and I placed my hand out as before and the feather floated down gently into my palm. I closed my hand around it, turned my eyes toward the Heavens and said "Thank you Lord!"

Now there were two feathers in the picture frame. Four years later, I was part of a small group for "Christian Singles" in the church I was attending. This particular evening was difficult for me as I was flooded with memories of my son after explaining the story to one of the other members. When it was time to leave, I remember being overwhelmed with grief and trying to hide my feelings from those around me. Just then, after I put on my leather jacket, I reached into one of the pockets and found a third feather! This was not a down jacket, and the feather was not in the pocket before our meeting. Nobody else there had heard the feather story before, or could have possibly known. I held onto the feather and when I reached my truck, started sobbing deeply. God knew how to reach me at just the right moment, in just the right way!

These feathers were tangible evidence that God knew how I was feeling and He decided to send me proof! There is absolutely no doubt in my mind that I experienced miracles from God. I still have those feathers saved in that same picture frame today! If you have been wondering what the feathers in the left margin represent, notice that they are shaped in a cross!

The voicemail from Heaven

Recently after my sister went to be with the Lord, my wife and I experienced a miraculous event we simply refer to as the voicemail from Heaven. One Saturday morning before receiving the news of my sister's passing. I picked up my cell phone which was beeping with a new voicemail message. There was a saved message that replayed before we could retrieve the new message that was waiting. The saved message from my sister, dated 3 weeks earlier, had never dropped down from the master voicemail system. She said "This is your beautiful sister calling, and I am having a lovely day." After playing this message on the speaker for my wife to hear, it was immediately followed by the new message from my

Dad explaining that my sister had gone Home to be with the Lord earlier that morning. We nearly dropped the phone, as we realized that my sister had just told us in her own words and voice, that she was ok and having a 'lovely day' in her new home in Heaven! How awesome was that?

> *"Hope and new beginnings are fresh every morning."*

One of my favorite explanations of hope is by Laura Lewis Lanier, who wrote "Hope and new beginnings are fresh every morning. It is not necessary to wait for a circumstance to bring hope. Hope, real hope, comes when we lay down our own ideas and plans... our mind, will, and emotions... before God as a hand of cards dealt, and say to Him, "How would YOU play them?"

Fresh Perspective

Recently, I had a vision that impacted me very deeply. I was meditating during my prayer time and had envisioned Jesus inviting me into heaven after my death. He said to me "Welcome home, I have someone here who has been waiting to see you!" And just then, I peek around the side of Jesus, and my son comes running to me and we embrace! It was so amazingly clear to me and so vivid that it has provided lasting comfort. It was such a powerful feeling that it took me several months before I could even share this vision with anyone else without sobbing! Today, when I want to stir up that hope within, all I need to do is close my eyes and replay the image of that beautiful vision. What a precious gift!

Hang onto your HOPE!

Simple Truth:

God knows us better than we know ourselves, and He always knows what we need and when we need it.

Faith Tip:

By opening our minds to God, we can see His hand at work in our personal lives through circumstances, events and people.

Encouraging News!

Memory Verse:
May the God of hope fill you with all joy and Peace as you trust in Him, so that you may overflow with hope by the power of the Holy Spirit. (Romans 15:13) NIV

My Journal:

What does this subject or scripture reading make you think or feel?

Chapter 15

Growing Our Faith

The subject of faith is near and dear to my heart because it is the very thing that pulled me through a deep depression from this tragic event in my life. Faith can pull you through too.

Early on when we began this medical journey with my son, if you had asked me if I had a strong faith I would surely have said "yes." However, I have learned that untested faith my not be nearly as strong as we think it is. Faith is described in the Bible as the <u>substance</u> of things hoped for and the evidence of things not seen. (see Hebrews 11:1)

Faith is a verb. That is how it is "the substance." It is not a feeling. It's a doing. It is our decision to think and act with confidence in God and His goodness. Faith is like a muscle. Through exercising faith over and over and building it by studying scripture it can be grown to the point where it feels unshakable. And faith will be tested. Faith is a requirement to endure difficult situations in our lives. Remember though, that one cannot have faith unless they first have hope. The primary reason for this book is to encourage hurting people to rediscover hope in their lives in order to strengthen faith and recover from whatever situation life has dealt them.

Undoubtedly, there were numerous instances where my faith had been tested during my son's journey through his liver transplantation. I remember at the beginning of that journey, I said to myself "this won't be too bad, he will just have the surgery and everything will be normal again." Fat chance! It was only the starting point of a very painful, lengthy and arduous battle.

Sometimes in life we imagine that things will be easier than they actually turn out to be. When we eventually realize how difficult something has become, we can lean on our faith to pull us through.

It is essential for faith to be tested and stretched to the very limits in order to grow. When our lives are humming along smoothly, it can become tempting to rely on ourselves and not seek God's hand or His strength as often. But when we hit a bump in the road, it shakes us up and then we may question if our faith is strong enough to endure. Unfortunately, it can take some huge bumps and very serious life-and-death scenarios to shake us to the point of asking God for help! When we do finally cry out to God, He jumps into action, stirs up our faith, and provides the necessary support to build our faith up to a new level. In a perfect world we may be able to grow our faith without this testing and proving. But it is almost impossible to strengthen it any other way.

> **"If God is your Co-Pilot then you better change seats!"**

In my own life I have endured many tough situations that have increased my faith even after my son's death. Sometimes it seems that was only the beginning; meaning that those events shook me up enough to get my attention. Once I realized and admitted that I was not strong enough on my own, God stepped in and started to work things out in my life. Basically, I just got out of the way and let Him take the wheel for a while. It sounds so simple but can be extremely difficult to someone who believes that they have their act together. It takes a portion of humility to admit that we need help and cannot endure things on our own. Yet when we do God takes action! Remember the bumper sticker that read " if God is your Co-Pilot then you better change seats!" Talk about right on the money!

A powerful tool for building your faith is to remember every time that God pulled you through other serious trials in life. This can and will help your faith grow. It helps you realize that God is there with you and will provide everything you need to weather the storm!

One thing I learned many years ago is that the staff that Moses, raised to the sky before God performed any miracle through him, was marked with engravings which identified previous miracles that God had performed. In essence what the Israelites were saying is "God, we know you have come through for us before and we are trusting that You will again." Remembering how God has helped you before is critical to building faith. You must remember everything God has helped you overcome and trust that He will help you endure your next trial no mater how enormous it may seem! If you have never previously permitted God to be a part of your life, you can build faith by reading and learning about the countless and amazing things He has done for others who rely on Him. The Bible is filled with true accounts of God rescuing people, and it's the best place to begin.

> **"God loves me enough to allow me the freedom to make healthy choices while rescuing me from being destroyed by my poor decisions."**

Sometimes I visualize our relationship with God this way: Hold your hands out in front of you with your palms facing each other and about 12 inches apart. Now imagine that they are God's hands and visualize Him holding us in His hands while allowing us to move back and forth between them. What this symbolizes to me is that God allows me to make decisions and choices on my own, but only within certain limits. If I step out too far in one direction or another, God is there to gently move me back the other way before I get into too much trouble. If I listen to Him, things work well. When I do something against His direction, I always encounter trouble eventually. As soon as I say "God, I am sorry I refused to do it Your way, please help me." He comes to my rescue.

What I like about this illustration is that God loves me enough to allow me the freedom to make healthy choices while rescuing me from being destroyed by my poor decisions.

Always keep in mind that God is the *only* perfect parent and will *never* mislead you. So even when your faith is being stretched to the very limits, remember that God is there waiting for you to ask Him for the help you need to endure and overcome any situation.

Fresh Perspective

Another visualization exercise I use is to remember that when I reach my hands to the sky and ask God for help, my hands are open. What this means is that I cannot hold anything else in my hands at the same time, which forces me to lay everything down at His feet before I raise my hands to ask for any request.

Remember to read and meditate on God's Word. You cannot expect to grow in faith without help from the Word of God. Read and meditate on the scriptures daily to feed your faith, and God will reveal Himself to you in a most powerful and present way.

Simple Truth:

Always keep in mind that God is the <u>only</u> perfect parent and will <u>never</u> mislead you.

Faith Tip:

Imagine your loved one in the paradise of Heaven and both of you being re-united with the Father someday – This can bring lasting peace and comfort just knowing where they are and that you will be there also.

Encouraging News!

Memory Verse:

So do not fear, for I am with you; do not be dismayed, for I am your God. I will strengthen you, and help you; I will uphold you with my righteous right hand. (Isaiah 41:10) NIV

My Journal:

What does this subject or scripture reading make you think or feel?

_____

_____

_____

_____

_____

_____

_____

_____

_____

_____

_____

_____

_____

_____

_____

_____

_____

_____

_____

_____

Chapter 16

Overcoming Grief, Guilt and Shame

Many years later, I still am only now learning the differences when it comes to grief, guilt and shame. Each one is a very different type of emotion. Grief is directly related to the loss and the pain and emptiness we feel. Grief is a normal part of the process when someone dies. Guilt and shame however, can be destructive in our lives if we do not deal with these thoughts and feelings early on. We must get to the truth of the matter and deal with it openly, because guilt and shame have the power to destroy you, if you let them.

Out of the blue my son's body had been overtaken by some disease, as his immune system was deliberately suppressed to avoid liver rejection after his recent transplantation. Very near the end, he was laying in a hospital bed medically paralyzed; sedated; on dialysis because his kidneys stopped functioning; his heart swollen to 4 times larger than normal; suffering occasional seizures; having (suspected) brain damage; and was connected to 9 intravenous pumps with a total of 15 medications coursing through his little body. It was the worst situation he had ever been in since both of his liver transplantations, seizures, or subsequent surgeries over the previous 1 ½ years. We met with a team of doctors on several occasions to brainstorm any options that were available and at one point, even tried experimental medications. When all of these things failed, our family was faced with the horrifying question… Do we give up? Is there still hope? After many tears and much deliberation, we unanimously decided to stop the medications and equipment that was artificially keeping him alive. It was by far the most gut-wrenching decision any of us had ever had to make. But together, we felt that at this point if God wanted Bobby to survive then He would save him without the medications and equipment which were artificially keeping his body alive.

I spent much time in prayer before and after this decision, and felt an unexplainable peace with whatever was going to happen. It seemed like everyone was at peace with it at the time. It is hard to put into words, but after so many days, weeks, and even years dealing with life and death situations there was a part of me that was beyond exhaustion. I will never understand how Bobby dealt with the trauma of all the surgeries, bandages, needles and medications as well as he did. It was inspirational to me that if he could deal with this, then so could I.

That said, there was still an enduring yearning deep inside of me for things to be normal... We had gone so far beyond "normal" for such a long time, I had no idea of what it even looked like anymore! It was as though my thoughts were switched to auto-pilot, which seemed to bring a certain amount of comforting numbness to the reality I faced daily.

Once the decision to let him go had been made, the hospital took steps to make us all feel at ease, as everyone was out of suggestions - especially the doctors. They removed some of the equipment that was artificially keeping his body alive while they kept supplying medicine to help Bobby stay comfortable until he passed away only a few hours later.

A few days later after the funeral was over and everyone had gone home, I started to question our decision. Were we right? Was there anything else we could have done? The questions were tormenting and I felt overwhelmed as this rush of guilt flooded my mind. What I didn't know at the time was that these thoughts were an attack by Satan to use guilt to make me feel shame on the deepest level. It was several years later before I realized this. So, I lived with a constant feeling of guilt and shame for the first few years, and was afraid to talk about it with anyone. Now that Bobby's mother and her parents were gone from my life, who could I trust and more importantly… who could understand what I was feeling?

> ## *"God does not make us feel shameful. or condemned."*

The truth which I have learned over time is that God <u>does not</u> make us feel shameful or condemned. It is the enemy who bombarded my thoughts with these cruel doubts. His goal is to steal, kill, and destroy, and he was trying to do that to me. In John 10:10 (NKJV) the Bible says *"The thief does not come except to steal, kill, and destroy. I have come that they may have life, and that they may have it more abundantly."* Satan uses shame as a weapon to make us feel defeated, worthless, and alone.

God uses the Holy Spirit to convict us when we need correction. But it is the enemy who condemns us if we believe his lies. But we don't need to believe his lies! Don't let tormenting thoughts remain in your mind! Replace them quickly and pray. God can and will protect you if you ask Him! In Revelation 12:10 the Bible says *"Then I heard a loud voice saying in Heaven, Now salvation, and strength, and the kingdom of our God, and the power of His Christ have come, for the accuser of our brethren, who accused them before our God day and night has been cast down."* You see, Satan <u>has been defeated</u>!

Reflecting back on our decision, I remember that God was part of it and He was there with us throughout the whole experience. I had to keep reminding myself of this truth and trust that God had guided our decision – even though at the time we did not know why, or how it fit, or what sense it could ever make.

Fresh Perspective

Years later I finally came to the realization and have absolutely no doubt whatsoever that God has used this event in my life to bring me to Him and help me to see what kind of work He wants me to do while I am here. You see, tragedy can really define a person's life. But I believe that what really matters is what you do with it. Do you decide to wallow in your own sorrow or self-pity? Or do you help others in similar situations to overcome their grief?

I believe that God inspired me to write this book. Initially it was for my own recovery and later to use it to reflect what He wants said to help others identify with the words for healing. When you can put yourself in this story, and begin to use the suggested tools, you will have a guide for recovery - and your heart can heal at last.

Simple Truth:

God is always with me and understands my every thought, and my every pain.

Faith Tip:

Create a "Gratitude List" and choose to focus on the good things God has provided for you and meditate on His goodness.

Encouraging News!

Memory Verse:

Therefore, there is now no condemnation for Those who are in Christ Jesus, because through Christ Jesus the law of the Spirit of life set me free from the law of sin and death. (Romans 8:1-2) NIV

My Journal:

What does this subject or scripture reading make you think or feel?

_____

_____

_____

_____

_____

_____

_____

_____

_____

_____

_____

_____

_____

_____

_____

_____

_____

_____

_____

_____

_____

_____

Chapter 17

Experiencing Peace with God's Plan

While I was prayer-running a few months ago, I believe that The God revealed something that was shockingly simple, but very healing to me. The summary of that thought is this: If I believe that God really is in control of _everything_ in my life, I must then also believe that He chose that particular moment and method to bring my son home to Him. Therefore, regardless of the circumstances, it was permitted to happen this way and I must not hold any resentment toward the people who were involved; regardless of their part in this situation.

At that very moment I realized that I was still holding onto some resentment toward the doctors who misdiagnosed and overmedicated my son, which lead to the necessity for liver transplantation in the first place. This was a huge insight for me! Once it was revealed, I immediately started praying out loud for the release of any unforgiveness or resentments that I was holding onto. Words cannot sufficiently explain just how freeing this moment was. It always amazes me that when we are in that "right state of mind" to receive God's insights, He provides them in the clearest manner!

> *"Healing also comes from being connected with other people who share my faith."*

I have found that healing also comes from being connected with other people who share a common faith, especially in small groups. Over the last ten years I have participated in several study and recovery groups and even lead a few. Through book studies which also reference the Bible and related discussions, my faith has grown tremendously. Also, any good group will promote trust by keeping personal details confidential, which can also provide for good mutual accountability.

I strongly encourage you to seek out a faith-based group to connect with that provides a safe environment in which to share your thoughts and experiences. It will give you the comfort of knowing you are not in this life alone and can be a source of life-changing insights and relationships. Be wise in selecting a group. Remember the guidelines provided in earlier chapters to protect yourself until the group proves to be trustworthy. At this writing, we are just beginning to offer some resources for this. Please visit us at www.hopetheothersideofgrief.com for additional resources and recovery tools.

Fresh Perspective

Over the years it has been very healing for me to share the story of how my son brought me to Jesus through his death. Actually, just by writing this statement I realized how similar that is to Jesus dying to bring us to the Father. Wow, is God amazing! He is always Good!

I encourage you to pursue peace through a divine connection with God. He has a good plan for your life; and by staying connected with Him you can discover newfound joy and purpose!

Simple Truth:

All we really need is God and time to heal our broken heart.

Faith Tip:

Getting involved in some type of support group can provide much needed rest for the soul and facilitate the opportunity to share your story with caring people.

Encouraging News!

Memory Verse:

Now we know that if the earthly tent we live in is destroyed, we have a building from God, an eternal house in Heaven, not built by human hands. (2 Corinthians 5:1) NIV

My Journal:

What does this subject or scripture reading make you think or feel?

_____

_____

_____

_____

_____

_____

_____

_____

_____

_____

_____

_____

_____

_____

_____

_____

_____

_____

_____

Chapter 18

Walking In Victory

Walking in victory simply means to stay healthy in your spirit, mind, will, and emotions with a definite understanding of who you are and that you have a purpose in this life! The following bullet points describe some important truths for you to remember and meditate on:

* Always remember that God is still in control and that nothing is a surprise to Him. Everything that happens in our lives, good and bad, He can use for your good if you work with Him! Romans 8:28 (NIV) says "And we know that in all things God works for the good of those who love Him, who have been called to His purpose."

* If you stay open to Him, God will reveal Himself in many ways to you daily. These gentle reminders from Him can bring you comfort – they definitely have to me!

* God has something GREAT in store for you and it is better than you can ask or even imagine!

Recently, I was praying and was very unclear about what the subject of the last chapter in this book should be. Then, out of the blue, God revealed to me that I should share this story with you as a reminder to hang on to your faith and hope. When we do this God can perform miracles!

When my current wife was 17 years old, she made a very wise decision to give her newborn baby girl up for a closed adoption. She never really questioned herself on this decision, as she felt like God was there guiding and comforting her, even in the midst of the turmoil of her situation and all those around her. Her landlady and employer were doing their best to convince her to get an abortion. She was a runaway from a very abusive family, but still had a sense of who God was and that He had better things in store for her life than she'd experienced as a child. She recognized that she was only 17 and all alone and that she could give neither herself or her child a good life.

Fast-forward 29 years to find us initiating an outreach to her daughter; her only child. What we discovered was that her daughter had the same desire in her heart and longed to meet her birth mother. In fact, her daughter was so excited, that in her first letter she invited my wife to come and hold her grandchildren!

The real significance in this story is that before we married we made a decision to not have any children due to her health and my unwillingness to risk losing another child. Since she did not know any details about her daughter; and my son had died as a toddler, it made grandchildren an impossibility - or so we thought!

> *"Who would ever have dreamed that this would be possible?...God did."*

God is so good and a God of miracles! He wants good things for His children. The real difference though, is that His idea of good things can be so much better than we could ever expect! Today we are proud Grandparents! Who would ever have dreamed that this would be possible?...God did. We cannot give Him enough praise for what He has and is doing for us! His plans are so incredibly good! It is challenging to explain just how life-changing this development is to us. I remember feeling like I was in a pit after my son died, and thought many times that life for me was pretty much over. Now take another look. I am an active Christ follower who has lead a men's prayer group, is active in my church, manages a very successful God-owned construction business, is an

Author and Support Group Leader, and now… a Grandpa! Our God can do anything! Do not give up. If God can do this for me, He can do it for you. Just give Him a chance and watch the amazing things He will do for you!

I want to end this book with this powerful and positive message. **Our** God is bigger than any problems, any grief, any disaster, or broken-life. ***He can and will save anyone who opens their heart and life to Him through His Son Jesus Christ!*** If you want even more proof of how God works, just take the first step and ask Jesus to come into your heart and take control of your life. In short order you will come to realize for yourself just how powerful and wonderful our God is and that He will take excellent care of you. He loves you. You are His precious child! Meditate on that, and let your healing begin.

God Bless you and your family!

SUMMARY

This book serves as a testament to God. May He work through the words it contains to reach people when they are hurting deeply in order to bring them into a new or deeper relationship with Him. The emphasis of this book is not intended to simply be a story about a man or his son; but rather a story of new found hope and restoration through turning to our Creator when we need Him the most! One day I realized that what I was feeling about my own loss, was but a portion of how it must have been for God to give up His precious Son, Jesus and the severe pain that He must have felt while His Son was being falsely accused and brutally crucified. We have a God who truly understands our pain.

After years of writing, healing, and growing in my own spiritual life, I realized that hope is the first key element which can lead to faith and eventually to healing. It has been said a number of times that a person cannot have faith if they first do not have hope. I believe this to be true and significant. Because the loss becomes a defining point in peoples' lives, where they either have hope and can start to heal; or hope eludes them and they flounder around in the thick black clouds of grief, depression, and emotional turmoil.

It is my heart's cry to reach hurting people at this most critical point when they question everything in their lives, especially God. This can be the most opportune moment to share hope with someone who is hurting and become part of their transformation from grief to hope. ***This is the very point at which God can take someone's deepest tragedy and turn it into their greatest triumph!***

This verse in scripture sums up the very essence of why this book exists and what I believe Christ has called me to do for others:

Praise be to the God and Father of our Lord Jesus Christ, the Father of compassion and the God of all comfort, who comforts us in all our troubles, so that we can comfort those in any trouble with the comfort we ourselves have received from God.

2 Corinthians 1:3-4

May all that I say and do bring glory to You Lord!

APPENDIX

"Simple Truths" Listed in each chapter:

1. We do not know how many days we have together. So we must treasure every memory each day brings.
2. God is with you at every level of your faith, and what He wants for you is to move to higher levels.
3. We may feel all alone, but the truth is that we are never really alone at all.
4. It is important to remember that we are never truly alone, even though it feels like it at the time!
5. God meets us where we are… He never Judges us and He does not hold our past mistakes against us.
6. My life has not ended, my life with You (God) it's just beginning…
7. By sharing your story with trusted friends in a safe small group environment, you can release the burden you have been carrying and really can begin the healing process.
8. God is working through me in the lives of others.
9. Recounting good memories in a balanced amount/way can provide comfort and promote healing.
10. Our faith is strengthened by passing through the tests in life, both the good and the painful.
11. Get alone with God and He will provide everything you need to heal and be restored.
12. Miracles are happening all around us, Can you see them?
13. God will hold you and comfort you like nobody else can – Trust Him.
14. God knows us better than we know ourselves, and He always knows what we need and when we need it…
15. Always keep in mind that God is the <u>only</u> perfect parent and will <u>never</u> mislead you.
16. God is always with me and understands my every thought, and my every pain.
17. All we really need is God and time to heal our broken heart.

"Faith Tips" Listed in each chapter:

1.   When times are seemingly at their worst and you are tempted to blame God, invite Him in and ask for comfort, strength and guidance for your heart, mind, and spirit – He will surely provide.
2.   When tragedy strikes, it is important to not blame God. These are times to lean on Him the most!
3.   Surrounding yourself with others frequently can ease your pain and give you something to look forward to – there is no room for sadness, when others are lifting you up!
4.   Sometimes humming a favorite hymn or song can keep fear at bay and remind you that   God is close by
5.   Try a change of scenery… Changing your inner circle of friends can bring you to a higher standard
6.   Developing a humble heart and accepting help that only God can give will bring us back to Him and can provide a renewed sense of peace in our lives.
7.   Seeking out a small group or life group at a local church, surrounding yourself with other Believers, praying and reading your Bible daily can bring healing to your soul.
8.   By helping others in the middle of their difficulties, not only does it take our attention off ourselves, but can also provide peace and healing through our gratitude.
9.   It can be important to some people in their healing process to determine a healthy way of remembering those who were important and provide hope that they will be reunited some day.
10.   This side of Heaven we may never understand, But we can trust the heart of our caring, loving, and compassionate God and know we're always in His hands.
11.   Speak declarations and scripture verses out-loud daily during your prayer time.
12.   God is always at work in your life and He smiles when you turn your eyes toward Him.
13.   Finding some new ways of celebrating holidays can be

helpful, possibly even traveling to different destinations – try something new!

14. By opening our minds to God, we can see His hand at work in our personal lives through circumstances, events and people.

15. Imagine your loved one in the paradise of Heaven and both of you being re-united with the Father someday – This can bring lasting peace and comfort just knowing where they are and that you will be there also.

16. Create a "Gratitude List" and choose to focus on the good things God has provided for you and meditate on His goodness.

17. All we really need is God and time to heal our broken heart.

"Encouraging News" Scripture Memory Verse Listed in each chapter:

1. As the heavens are higher than the earth, so are my ways higher than your ways and my thoughts higher than your thoughts. Isaiah 55.9

2. Lord You are good, and Your mercies endureth forever! Psalm 100:5

3. For I am the Lord your God who takes hold of your right hand and says to you, do not fear, I will help you. Isaiah 41:13

4. God is our refuge and strength, and ever-present help in trouble. Psalm 46:1

5. Set you minds on things above, not on earthly things. Colossians 3:2

6. Blessed is the man whose sin the Lord will never count against him. Romans 4:8

7. And hope does not disappoint us, because God has poured out his love into our hearts by the Holy Spirit, whom he has given us. Romans 5:5

8. The Lord is good, a refuge in times of trouble. He cares for those who trust in him. Nahum 1:7

9. My comfort in my suffering is this: Your promise preserves my life. Psalm 119:50

10. We live by faith and not by sight. 2 Corinthians 5:7

11. I can do all things through Christ who gives me the strength. Philippians 4:13

12. Set your minds on things above, not on earthly things. Colossians 3:2

13. Praise be to the God and Father of our Lord Jesus Christ, the Father of compassion and the God of all comfort, who comforts us in all our troubles, so that we can comfort those in any trouble with the comfort we ourselves have received from God. 2 Corinthians 1:3-4

14. May the God of hope fill you with all joy and peace as you trust in Him, so that you may overflow with hope by the power of the Holy Spirit. Romans 15:13

15. So do not fear, for I am with you; do not be dismayed, for I am your God. I will strengthen you, and help you; I will uphold you with my righteous right hand.   Isaiah 41:10

16. Therefore, there is now no condemnation for those who are in Christ Jesus, because through Christ Jesus the law of the Spirit of life set me free from the law of sin and death. Romans 8:1-2

17. Now we know that if the earthly tent we live in is destroyed, we have a building from God, an eternal house in Heaven, not built by human hands. 2 Corinthians 5:1

Made in the USA
Monee, IL
21 November 2021